BUILDERS OF THE ANCIENT WORLD

Marvels of Engineering

Prepared by the Special Publications Division
National Geographic Society, Washington, D.C.

BLAINE HARRINGTON III (BELOW); PAGE 1: ADAM WOOLFITT/WOODFIN CAMP, INC.; PAGES 2-3: DAVID ALAN HARVEY

CONTENTS

BUILDERS OF THE ANCIENT WORLD
Marvels of Engineering

Contributing Authors: RON FISHER, NORMAN HAMMOND,
   ANN NOTTINGHAM KELSALL, JOYCE STEWART,
   GENE S. STUART
Contributing Photographers: WILLIAM ALBERT ALLARD,
   DEAN CONGER, RICHARD A. COOKE III,
   BLAINE HARRINGTON III, STEVE MCCURRY

Published by THE NATIONAL GEOGRAPHIC SOCIETY
   GILBERT M. GROSVENOR, *President*
   MELVIN M. PAYNE, *Chairman of the Board*
   OWEN R. ANDERSON, *Executive Vice President*
   ROBERT L. BREEDEN, *Senior Vice President,*
      Publications and Educational Media

Prepared by THE SPECIAL PUBLICATIONS DIVISION
   DONALD J. CRUMP, *Director*
   PHILIP B. SILCOTT, *Associate Director*
   BONNIE S. LAWRENCE, *Assistant Director*

Staff for this Book
   MARY ANN HARRELL, *Managing Editor*
   THOMAS B. POWELL III, *Illustrations Editor*
   CINDA ROSE, *Art Director*
   JODY BOLT, *Consulting Art Director*
   PENELOPE DIAMANTI DE WIDT, *Senior Researcher*
   ELIZABETH B. BOOZ, VICTORIA GARRETT CONNORS,
      PATRICIA F. FRAKES, LISE MCLEAN OLNEY, *Researchers*
   SEYMOUR L. FISHBEIN, RON FISHER, ALICE K. JABLONSKY,
      H. ROBERT MORRISON, GENE S. STUART,
      PAMELA BLACK TOWNSEND, *Picture Legend Writers*
   SUSAN SANFORD, *Map Art and Production*
   VIRGINIA L. BAZA, JOSEPH F. OCHLAK, *Map Research*
   WELLER, FISHBACK & BOHL, Architects:
      DOUGLAS A. RISCH, *Artist for Drawings*
   ARTEMIS S. LAMPATHAKIS, *Illustrations Assistant*

Engraving, Printing, and Product Manufacture
   ROBERT W. MESSER, *Manager*
   DAVID V. SHOWERS, *Production Manager*
   GEORGE J. ZELLER, JR., *Production Project Manager*
   GREGORY STORER, *Senior Assistant Production Manager*
   MARK R. DUNLEVY, *Assistant Production Manager*
   TIMOTHY H. EWING, *Production Assistant*
   MARY F. BRENNAN, VICKI L. BROOM, CAROL ROCHELEAU
      CURTIS, LORI E. DAVIE, MARY ELIZABETH DAVIS,
      ANN DI FIORE, ROSAMUND GARNER,
      BERNADETTE L. GRIGONIS, VIRGINIA W. HANNASCH,
      NANCY J. HARVEY, JOAN HURST, KATHERINE R. LEITCH,
      ANN E. NEWMAN, CLEO E. PETROFF, STUART E. PFITZINGER,
      VIRGINIA A. WILLIAMS, *Staff Assistants*
   DIANNE L. H. HARDY, *Indexer*

*PAGE 1: Standing-stone arrays at Carnac, in France, evoke
enigmas of prehistory. PAGES 2-3: Maya shrines at Tulum hold
echoes of New World civilization. OPPOSITE: Children at
Hadrian's Villa learn of imperial Rome.*

INTRODUCTION

INTRODUCTION

By Norman Hammond

T he profile of the whole stupendous ruin, as seen at a distance of a mile eastward, is clearly cut as that of a marble inlay. It is varied with protuberances, which . . . have the animal aspect of warts, wens, knuckles and hips. It may indeed be likened to an enormous many-limbed organism of an antediluvian time . . . lying lifeless and covered with a thin green cloth."

Thus novelist Thomas Hardy, looking from the window of his home near Dorchester in southern England, envisioned the massive earthworks of Maiden Castle, the great Iron Age fortress built on a nearby hilltop by the ancient Britons in the centuries before the Roman Conquest.

That conquest, an invasion in A.D. 43 led by the god-Emperor Claudius, was dramatically revealed half a century ago by the excavations of my old friend and mentor, Sir Mortimer Wheeler.

"As we dug on we came upon rough hollows: in each lay a human skeleton, sometimes two, in all manner of contortions, with all the semblance of having been slung carelessly into their crude graves. The skulls of many of them had been hacked viciously . . . one of them bore no less than nine deep cuts. The wounds were battle-wounds: one skull showed the square piercing of a Roman ballista-bolt, whilst another skeleton—most vivid relic of all—had an iron arrow-head embedded deeply in a vertebra."

Sir Mortimer was one of the greatest archaeologists of this century. His vivid description of the fall of Celtic Britain to the Romans made the past come alive for thousands of people—I was one of them, and it settled my choice of career at an early age. Not long after hearing him speak, I visited Maiden Castle on a high school trip. As I climbed those swelling green ramparts, not only did the final battle refight itself in my mind's eye, but I also acquired a healthy respect for the anonymous tribesmen who had turned this hill into such a stronghold. Proof against Roman legions it may not have been, but it must have deterred local aggressors with its triple ditches, steep scarps, and mazelike gateways studded with towers and sling-wielding sharpshooters.

Some two thousand years more recent than Stonehenge, the hill-forts of the Iron Age are the culmination of a long tradition of ambitious building works in this remote island at the edge of the then known world. They have their origins a millennium before Stonehenge, five thousand years ago, not long after the first farmers settled in southern England. Like other masterworks featured in this book, they reveal more than the technology of the past—they help us understand patterns of social life

PRECEDING PAGES: Memorials to Egyptian kings, the pyramids of Giza still rise above the desert after 4,000 years. Builders may have used water-filled ditches as a check on levels. Stone—not sun-dried mud brick—promised permanence for these monuments, only survivors of the ancient world's classic seven wonders.

1600—				last independent Inca executed 1572		Qing (Manchu) Dynasty 1644–1911
	Great Zimbabwe c. 1450	fall of Roman Empire in the East 1453	Spanish conquest begins 1519	Spanish conquest begins 1532 Inca Empire c. 1438–1532	Mogul Empire dominant in India 1526–mid-1700s	
1400—			Mexica (Aztecs) found city of Tenochtitlán c. 1325	bronze in use c. 1400 Chimu c. 1350–1470		Ming Dynasty 1368–1644 Yuan (Mongol) Dynasty 1279–1368
1000—	Easter Island statues c. 1100–1680 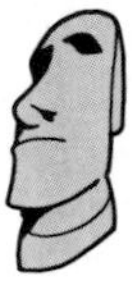		collapse of Classic Maya civilization c. 900–1000 Toltec civilization c. 800–1100	 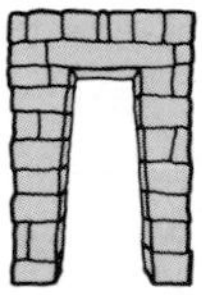	Khmer Empire in Southeast Asia c. 800–1430 Muslim conquests in subcontinent begin after 712	Song Dynasty 960–1279 suppression of Buddhism 840s
500—	Ctesiphon c. 300–600 Aksum 300–700	last Roman Emperor in the West deposed 476 Baths of Caracalla c. 212–216	Late Classic Maya c. 600–900 	Empire of Tiahuanaco c. 200–600	Hindu stone temples c. 400 to present	completion of Sui Grand Canal 589–610 spread of Buddhism c. 400–840s
100—	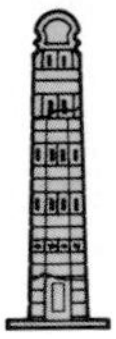	Roman Empire: greatest extent c. 117 Colosseum c. 70–c. 80 invasion of Britain 43	Teotihuacán c. 100–750	Moche culture c. A.D. 1–c. 750		
A.D. B.C.						
300—	Maiden Castle c. 250	 Epidaurus theater c. 350		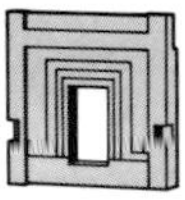	rock-cut architecture (c. 250 B.C.– A.D. 800) spread of Buddhism under Emperor Ashoka (c. 260–231)	Min River irrigation c. 200 B.C.–present Great Wall after c. 221 Qin Empire 221–207 iron in use c. 300
800—		Parthenon, Athens 447–32 Roman Republic 509–27 founding of Rome (traditional date) 753	Monte Albán c. 600 B.C.– A.D. 700	Chavín de Huántar c. 800	Siddhartha Gautama (the Buddha) ?563–?483 iron in use in north after 800	Warring States c. 475–221 Confucius 551–479
1500—	Poverty Point c. 1000 Stonehenge (sarsen circle) c. 1500	iron in use after c. 1000	Olmec culture c. 1200–400 		Aryan tribes settle in subcontinent c. 1500–500	
2800—	Ziggurat of Ur c. 2100 Great Pyramid c. 2600	bronze in use after c. 2800	Cuello c. 2400–A.D. 400		bronze in use in Indus Valley c. 2000 Indus (Harappan) civilization c. 2500–1800	bronze in use c. 2000
7500—	Stonehenge (earliest features) c. 3000 Çayönü c. 7000 Jericho c. 7500			earliest cultures c. 3000–2000		settled communities in Yellow River Valley c. 3500

(ILLUSTRATIONS ARE NOT POSITIONED BY TIME OF ORIGIN.)

found in many parts of the world, over a range of many centuries.

Last summer I stood on a sharp spur of the Cotswold Hills as Dr. Philip Dixon, a colleague from Nottingham University, told me of another battle long ago: "As you can see, Crickley Hill has steep drops on three sides, so the inhabitants only needed to fortify it on the north. They dug a series of quarry pits—right down there—and threw the dirt and rock up into a rampart, which held a timber palisade. Clearly, it was done by people expecting trouble. That came sometime around three thousand years before Christ, when Crickley was attacked with fire-arrows and destroyed. We have found literally hundreds of flint arrowheads along the line of the defenses; some were burnt and some had snapped, presumably where they hit hard timber."

Such an early beginning to warfare suggests that these pioneer farmers were already struggling for good land. Elsewhere in the British countryside we find hints of the territorial imperative in the form of megalithic tombs. As their name indicates, these use large stones—like those of Stonehenge, although usually smaller—to frame a burial chamber. This hollow house of the dead was buried below an impressive mound of earth and stones. Such "barrows" are found across Europe from Sweden to Spain, from Sardinia north to the Scottish islands.

Professor Colin Renfrew of Cambridge University has studied the distribution of these tombs in the Orkney Islands. He regards them as the territorial markers of tribal societies. He thinks that the labor invested in them was a public statement of communal purpose, including ownership and use of the land around. He has found interesting parallels in descriptions of stone monuments in the Tuamotu Islands, in the far-distant Pacific, where worship and feasting took place at chiefly burial sites—and when I visited the excavation of a tomb near Crickley Hill a few years ago, I found that the bones from an ancient pig roast had indeed been left lying near the entrance.

The most puzzling, and the most celebrated, of the megalithic monuments is Stonehenge, within 50 miles of both Maiden Castle and Crickley Hill, on the grassy Salisbury Plain. For hundreds of years the people of the region have come to marvel and make merry at the great stone circles. If any rested on a fallen stone, few can have realized what a complex piece of prehistoric engineering they were sitting on.

By authoritative estimates, more than 30 million man-hours went into building the final structure. At least that effort was needed to drag the 81 huge "sarsen" sandstones some 24 miles to the site. A further half million hours went into pounding the blocks into shape—the largest of them 30 feet high and weighing nearly 50 tons. Men gouged pits into the chalk bedrock, and evidently constructed ramps to slide the great stones into place; then the slabs were levered to an upright position and jammed into place with rocks. Finally, the lintels, nearly seven tons each, had to be raised twenty feet or more. Probably men pried up an end of the slab, fitted a square timber under it, lifted the other end the same way, added layer after layer of timber to make a "crib," and eventually edged the stone gingerly sideways onto the uprights. To keep the lintels in place the

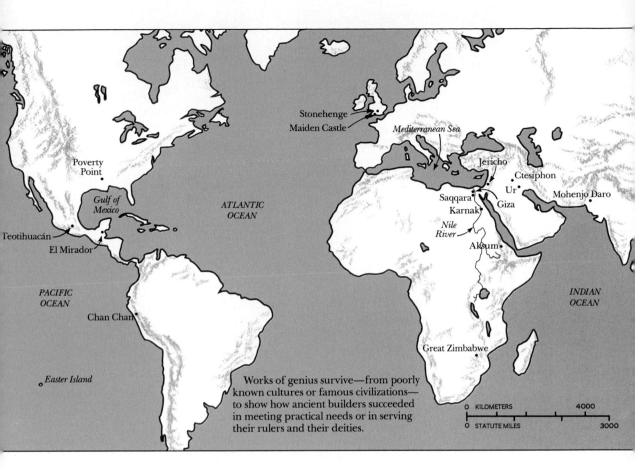

Stonehenge
Maiden Castle
Mediterranean Sea
Jericho
Ctesiphon
Poverty
Point
Ur
Mohenjo Daro
Gulf of
Mexico
ATLANTIC
OCEAN
Saqqara
Giza
Karnak
Nile
River
Teotihuacán
Aksum
El Mirador
PACIFIC
OCEAN
INDIAN
OCEAN
Chan Chan
Great Zimbabwe
Easter Island
Works of genius survive—from poorly
known cultures or famous civilizations—
to show how ancient builders succeeded
in meeting practical needs or in serving
their rulers and their deities.

KILOMETERS   4000
STATUTE MILES   3000

masons of Stonehenge used a carpenter's mortise-and-tenon joint—and
many other features suggest that the final Stonehenge was a wooden
monument translated into stone. Examples of such "woodhenges" have
been found nearby at the great earthwork enclosure of Durrington Walls,
where the estimated labor investment of nearly a million man-hours
attests the power of the local rulers and their ideology.

The reach of that power can be seen in an earlier Stonehenge as well.
Centuries before the sarsens were dragged together and pounded into
shape, slabs of blue dolerite were brought from the Prescelly Mountains
in southern Wales. As the crow flies it's a mere 140 miles, but rugged hills
and dangerous seas lie between. We believe that these builders of 2200
B.C. dragged the bluestones over the mountains, then brought them by
raft up the Bristol Channel to the river Avon. For the last stage the stones
would have been pulled on sledges—a generation ago Professor Richard
Atkinson harnessed a team of 32 high school seniors to a 3,000-pound slab
to prove that moving such rocks was not as hard as it might seem. He decided that the work needed, roughly, 16 men per ton. (I wonder if in fact
the builders harnessed not young men but oxen, since we know that they
had had domestic cattle for a thousand years. I can easily imagine bullocks
dragging a creaking sledge across the dew-slick grass.)

When I look at Stonehenge, or at the colossal mound of Silbury Hill not
far north—consumer of an estimated 18 million man-hours of continual

11

labor—and think of the relatively primitive technology and economy that lay behind them, I remember that other peoples in other lands have accomplished equally impressive feats of construction with no greater resources. One site that comes to mind is Great Zimbabwe, in southern Africa. Like Stonehenge, thought for a time to have been the work of a Greek architect, Great Zimbabwe is so impressive that white settlers assumed it must have been built by sophisticates from the Mediterranean. We now know it was the court of the Shona kings, rulers of modern Zimbabwe's most populous tribe, built in the 14th century A.D. and at its height in the 15th.

From the air it reveals curved stone walls, partially in ruin, scattered across low hills. Mud-walled houses stood here once, and the stone enclosures are an inspired translation of a mud corral into a permanent material—as Stonehenge transformed perishable wood into everlasting sarsen. At ground level, the great compound called the Elliptical Building is most impressive, with walls about 30 feet in height and half that in thickness. The tallest structure is a solid conical tower. It reproduces in stone the shape of a Shona granary; it proclaims the ruler's right to tribute and his duty to reward his people.

Archaeologist Peter Garlake calls this granite architecture "a creative human response to a marvelous natural building material." Its architect found truly elegant solutions to problems of design; the one which pleases me most is the continuation of wall courses as steps below a gap, each step curving gracefully outward to provide a tread.

The Shona lords had far-flung contacts. Through the Arab traders of the Indian Ocean they obtained Chinese celadon, Persian pottery, and glass from the Middle East. These finds were used more than half a century ago to establish the true age and native African inspiration of Great Zimbabwe; the insight was that of Gertrude Caton-Thompson, a peerless scholar who lived to see the ruins she had studied give their name to a new nation. She had come to southern Africa with a reputation firmly founded in the early archaeology of Egypt and Arabia.

In Asia tradition lies long in the dust. The age that separates us from ancient Ur, with its famous temple-tower ziggurat, is not so long as the age that separated Ur from the first builders of permanent dwellings. At Jericho, founded by a perennial spring in the Jordan Valley millennia before Joshua came trumpeting around its wall, there has been a community since the end of the last Ice Age. Over many generations its chief construction material, mud brick, accumulated into an impressive mound; the lowest levels held the houses of the Natufians, a people still getting their meat by hunting gazelles, but already relying on cereals—probably wild wheat and barley. The dirt floors of their small houses were pocked by shallow pits for storing grain and saddle-shaped stones for grinding it.

Jericho was obviously a place worth defending. Some 9,300 years ago its

Ant-like climbers scale exposed limestone blocks of the Great Pyramid at Giza. Armies of Egyptian workmen pulled these 15-ton blocks over a polished stone causeway to the construction site. Limestone cladding, cut to hundredths-of-an-inch perfection, originally gave each enormous triangular side an even slope.

inhabitants enclosed it with a wall of rough stone blocks, 14 feet high and more than 10 feet thick, perhaps 800 yards in circumference. At a strategic point stood a tower more than 25 feet high, a windowless cylinder of masonry with a narrow stair running up through its core.

Similar communities flourished farther east. Ten thousand years ago men were building round huts with red clay plaster at Tell Mureybit on the upper Euphrates River. About 7500 B.C. they took to building larger houses with neat square corners, while farming villages developed in what James Breasted once called with resonant accuracy "the Fertile Crescent." Flowing south across the curve of the crescent are the headwaters of the twin rivers Tigris and Euphrates, and high in the hills between them lies the site of Çayönü, where varied types of buildings were put up around 7000 B.C. Some have long parallel rooms on level dirt floors. Solid floors distinguish two larger structures; one is paved with flat flagstones as long as five feet, while the other has a striking orange-red floor with a mosaic of four kinds of limestone, all carefully polished. And in a third building, small cells contained clusters of human skulls. In contemporary Jericho, striking portraits were modeled in plaster over the bones of such skulls—perhaps in a cult venerating ancestors. Here, perhaps, we sense the inspiration for many great buildings of antiquity.

Five thousand years later these village cults had developed into the state-run religion of Sumer, first of civilizations. The house-size holy places had grown outward and upward to become the ziggurats, as low supporting platforms had been rebuilt time after time atop their predecessors. The shrine became the high holy of holies, enclosed within its own precinct in the heart of a walled city—the new way in which men had chosen to live.

Pride in these walls rings out in the ancient epic of Gilgamesh, one of the world's first poems set down in writing: Gilgamesh the king, "lord of wisdom . . . ordered built the walls of Uruk . . . the walls of holy Eanna, stainless sanctuary. Behold its inner wall, which no work can equal. Touch the stone threshold, which is ancient; draw near the Eanna, dwelling-place of the goddess Ishtar, a work no later kings can match. Ascend the walls of Uruk, walk around the top, inspect the base, view the brickwork. Is not the very core made of oven-fired brick?"

Not rubble, not sun-dried mud brick at the core, but weather-proof fired brick. Mud was there for the taking in the plain around Uruk, but trees were scarce; wood for the kilns would have been hauled in from great distances, at heavy cost. In the time of Gilgamesh, about 2600 B.C., the walls were six miles around. (He would have taken measurements in cubits and spans, a cubit being the distance from elbow to middle fingertip, a span from thumbtip to little fingertip on a hand stretched wide.) When his daring quest for immortality ended in defeat, he consoled himself with praise of his city and its noble walls. About a third of the city held

First of Egypt's great stone tombs, the Step Pyramid at Saqqara rises nearly 200 feet. Since about 2700 B.C. it has guarded the memory of King Djoser—and of its builder, Imhotep, one of the few architects known by name in world antiquity. Limestone columns (foreground) flank a ceremonial courtyard of his designing.

buildings, he said, a third orchards, a third claypits: "Three parts including the claypits make up Uruk."

Not far across the plain lies Ur, another of the early cities of Sumer, where the ziggurat built by King Ur-Nammu in 2100 B.C. owes the excellent condition of its remains to a casing of fired bricks set in bitumen. (This black tar, oozing out of the ground, led modern explorers to the oil wealth of Iraq.) To stabilize the mud-brick core of the ziggurat, workmen laced the interior with cables and mats of woven reeds. Ur remained a holy place a thousand years later, when the kings of Babylon—whose own great ziggurat is known to us as the Tower of Babel—took pride in maintaining this ancestral shrine. It was the home of the moon-god Nanna, and covered 30,000 square feet at ground level. From the summit, the architect could look out to the spreading city, or down to the storehouse,

ROGER WOOD/PICTUREPOINT — LONDON

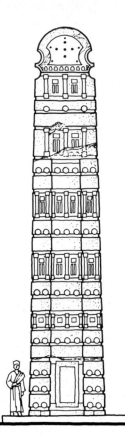

Fallen relic of Ethiopia's triumphal past intrigues a little girl at Aksum; the drawing shows it erect, a granite monolith of 110 feet above ground— a notable height in ancient times. Although Christianity reached Aksum by A.D. 327, these monuments may continue a pagan tradition; their exact purpose remains obscure. Perhaps they commemorate rulers. They may reflect knowledge of Egyptian obelisks a thousand years older, but the stelae of Aksum represent a style of their own, independent of influences from Upper Egypt and southern Arabia. The carving simulates windows, timbers, and the distinctive round protruding beams locally known as "monkeyheads"; Ethiopian architects have used these features for almost two thousand years.

priestesses' residence, and royal lodging enclosed within the precinct wall. He would call this sacred complex the *temen,* source of our word "temple." Evidently he worked from a scale drawing: Gudea of Lagash, the ruler of a neighboring city, had a sculptor portray him holding the plan of his temple, a plan remarkably like a modern blueprint.

The design had developed from simple origins. The alternating recesses and buttresses of Sumer's sacred buildings developed from the reed bundles, stood on end and bound together, used as structural materials to this day by the Marsh Arabs in the swampy delta of the twin rivers.

Power in Mesopotamia always depended on control of the water supply. Early rulers supervised the construction of canals to irrigate the dusty plains, and some of the world's oldest lawsuits deal with water rights. If the river moved away from a city, it died: Ur, once washed on two sides by the Euphrates, now molders in the desert.

Throughout the Middle East, men made ingenious schemes to bring water from the hills where it fell, to the flat lands where it could refresh the parched soil and sustain the cities. To me no device is more amazing in its precision than the *qanat,* which I have admired in operation from the Fertile Crescent east to the Turfan Depression in China. Qanats are long

Woodworker's joinery fitted the multi-ton slabs in the trilithons at Stonehenge about 1400 B.C. Each upright has two small knobs, or tenons, on top; each lintel has pits, or mortises, to match, plus tongue-and-groove joints at either end. Pounding this hard sarsen sandstone with a stone maul removes about six cubic inches of dust and sand an hour; shaping the slabs must have taken years.

tunnels, very gently graded like miniature subways, which reach from low-lying villages to tap the water table in the hills. The underground course preserves water that the sun would steal from surface channels. As early as 1240 B.C. a qanat "that brings abundance" served the Assyrian capital of Nimrud, with rock-cut tunnels along part of its course.

A famous, if inefficiently built, tunnel is the one at Jerusalem, cut from the Gihon spring to the pool of Siloam on the orders of Hezekiah, king of Judah, around 700 B.C. It was meant to frustrate an enemy siege. As the Bible's Second Book of Chronicles records (32:2-4), workmen said, "Why should the kings of Assyria come, and find much water?" A commemorative tablet tells the story—and it was put up with relief, I imagine, because the 366-yard distance had stretched into a wriggly tunnel more than 200 yards longer by the time Hezekiah's miners had joined their two projects in a mighty dogleg. "Whilst yet the miners were lifting up the pick, and there were three cubits to be cut through there was heard the voices of men calling to each other, for there was a split in the rock. When they met the miners struck pick upon pick . . . and a hundred cubits was the height of the rock above their heads."

No scribe sang the great qanat of Aleppo in Syria, seven and a half miles long, nor that of Irbil in Kurdistan, where three branches deliver a quarter of a million gallons a day. Yet they deserve praise, for like thousands of shorter ones they were built without the help of surveying instruments. Instead, a master tunneler would rely on seasoned judgment. At the base of the hills he would sink a shaft to the water table. Then he would dig vertical shafts 20 to 50 yards apart, on a course to the town or village. Diggers would cut their way from shaft to shaft, with a trickle of water from upstream as a guide, and finally would enlarge the highest link to increase the flow.

Qanat technology was taken to Egypt in 518 B.C. by Scylax, one of the naval captains of the Persian emperor Darius. Scylax found himself trapped out of water in both senses of the word, in the desert west of the Nile. He drove more than nine miles of tunnels, and when one of these was discovered in A.D. 1900 it was yielding about 40 gallons a minute.

The Persians were latecomers to Egypt, where the waters of the Nile had fed a civilization as great and as early as that of Mesopotamia. Recently I stood on the desert edge at Saqqara, looking out over the fields toward the site of Memphis, for centuries the Pharaohs' capital. I turned, my back to the river, to marvel at the zigzag profile of Djoser's stepped pyramid, the first monumental stone building in the world. Built about 2650 B.C., this revolutionary structure is an enduring memorial to two men. The first is Djoser, second ruler of Egypt's Third Dynasty; the other is his vizier Imhotep, who rose from a civil servant's family to become—as an ancient inscription says—"Chancellor of the King of Lower Egypt, First after the King of Upper Egypt, Administrator of the Great Palace,

Suavely curved steps in a wall 30 feet high reveal the originality of an unknown architect at Great Zimbabwe, the 100-acre site of spectacular ruins that inspired the name of a modern African nation. With local granite that fractures into cube-like blocks, and without mortar, masons built structures worthy of a ruler's court.

GEORG GERSTER

Hereditary Nobleman, High Priest of Heliopolis, Builder, Sculptor and Maker of Vases in Chief." Later Egyptians worshiped him as a god.

We remember Imhotep by the mighty tomb he built for his king and friend, and marvel at how a much-changed original design reached such a handsome conclusion. Excavations have shown that initially Djoser was to have had a traditional *mastaba* tomb: a burial chamber sunk into bedrock, and over it a structure shaped like a shoebox with walls slanting slightly inward. This mastaba was enlarged twice, then revised dramatically. It became, in appearance, a stack of platforms, its base some 350 by 400 feet and its height almost 200. More than three-quarters of a million tons of stone were used, laid not in flat platforms but in steep sloping walls that lean against each other like massive sets of books around a central core. The design was safe and stable, a proof of Imhotep's genius, copied in the later and larger pyramids of Egypt.

The day after I had enjoyed the fresh breeze at Saqqara, I was crawling through a locker-room dankness inside the Great Pyramid of Djoser's successor of the Fourth Dynasty, Cheops (or Khufu). The three pyramids of Giza are the one surviving Wonder of the Ancient World; the tallest now stands 482 feet at its summit. Yet they are much smaller than photographs had led me to expect. That surprising human dimension made

24

the engineering skill that had gone into them the more impressive. They date from the era when Gilgamesh was raising the burnt-brick walls of Uruk, and the first stones were being erected at Stonehenge; and their compact grandeur told me that Imhotep had worthy followers.

That pungency of air in Cheops' monument did not lessen my awe. From a low tunnel at the base I followed the steep upward slope of the Grand Gallery, under a vaulted roof lost in the low-wattage glow of naked lights. The royal burial chamber is small and plain, containing a small and plain sarcophagus for the king. As my friend John Ruffle once put it, "unsupported by any magical inscriptions or blazoned records of his mighty deeds, he calmly made the entry into eternity, assured of recognition and acceptance." The scale of his pyramid ensures that. Some of the blocks in the core exceed 200 tons, and some of the facing blocks, of fine limestone, exceed 30. Work gangs, an estimated 900 strong, dragged them up long earthen ramps and set them in place with near-absolute precision.

Preliminary work alone meant "ten years' oppression of the people," reported Herodotus, the Greek historian who visited Egypt as a tourist in the fifth century B.C. The site was leveled (apparently with a water-filled ditch around it as a reference), and a 1,000-yard causeway built for the conveyance of stones from the riverbank. It was, said Herodotus, "polished stone carved with figures of animals—no less a feat, in my opinion, than the pyramid itself." That required another 20 years, he noted, with 100,000 men working in three-month shifts. These figures, incidentally, seem quite reasonable: Commander F. M. Barber, a U.S. naval attaché abroad in the late 1800s, made a detailed study of the "mechanical triumphs" of the ancient Egyptians, and estimated that the energy which went into building the Great Pyramid would have powered a 10,000-ton steamship for 70 voyages around the globe at 20 knots.

With small wooden rafts and ships, Egyptian crews moved some of their ponderous blocks—and the far more demanding obelisks quarried at Aswan. There, in a hillside east of town, I found toolmarks as sharp as the day they were made more than 3,000 years ago, and an unfinished monument to ambition: an obelisk 135 feet long, abandoned when sharp eyes spotted a flaw in the rock. It took a long ship to carry such multi-ton monsters; and to keep bow and stern from drooping under the weight, men secured them to the obelisk itself with an ingenious truss of strong rope. Just such a "hog frame" was reinvented on the Mississippi in the 1800s, for big paddle steamers taking heavy loads in shallow waters.

Near Deir el-Bahri I passed two huge statues sitting in the fields, looking rather lonely: the so-called Colossi of Memnon, each 68 feet of solid stone. These were brought *upstream* from quarries near Cairo. Eight ships, pontoon rafts presumably, carried these thousand-ton loads; and by Barber's calculations, the 15,000 men needed to drag them overland

PRECEDING PAGES: *Built about 2100 B.C., now partly restored, the ziggurat of Ur honors its Sumerian creators. One of three tiers survived nearly intact— a core of sun-dried brick reinforced with reed mats and faced with fired brick.* OPPOSITE: *A stone plaque 4,500 years old depicts a Sumerian king, the great Ur-Nanshe of Lagash, carrying brick for a temple, then toasting its completion.*

would have occupied an area about 25 by 330 yards as they worked.

Here in Egypt we know the names not only of the rulers, but often of the architects, administrators, and overseers who carried out these amazing tasks. In contrast, the ancient civilization of the Indus Valley is utterly anonymous. It stretched from the foothills of the Himalayas to the Arabian Sea, from the borders of Iran to the center of India. But we do not know the name of a single ruler of its greatest cities—now called Harappa and Mohenjo Daro—which flourished between 2500 and 1800 B.C. Clearly someone planned these: At each, a citadel looms over a grid-planned lower town as regular in street pattern as Manhattan. Residential blocks shared a buried sewerage system, another proof of advance planning and good civil engineering.

And last summer I was one of a stunned audience in Arhus, Denmark, when my friends Michael Jansen and Maurizio Tosi, coleaders of a current project at Mohenjo Daro, reported their latest findings. They have been conducting a remarkable surface survey. Thousands of colored markers pinned down industrial areas in the southeast quarter of the city, while the team plotted each piece of scrap—copper slag, broken pottery, imperfect beads. Meanwhile a proton magnetometer detected different densities of buried mud-brick construction. These showed that one of the major residential areas had been developed on a huge platform, some 2,600 feet long, apparently built as a unit when the city was first laid out. The implications are breathtaking: Mohenjo Daro, thought to have held at least 40,000 people, did not grow gradually, like the cities of Mesopotamia, but was imposed upon the landscape. Perhaps it was the earliest pre-planned town in the world. "This changes the way we look at this city, Norman," Michael told me enthusiastically. "They had the whole thing in their minds at the very beginning!"

But who were they? As yet we cannot read the Indus script, and perhaps the most surprising aspect of these cities is the modesty which keeps

from us the images of their rulers. Sir Mortimer Wheeler dug at Mohenjo Daro in the 1940s, and found no tombs, no statues, to suggest who directed these grandiose, strangely modern projects.

While the Indus cities collapsed into anonymity, a massive new use of human labor was developing 2,500 miles to the east in China, in the valley of the Yellow River. There the first rulers of the Shang Dynasty were emerging from the mist of legendary origins. Not long ago I saw, and admired, one of their impressive monuments: the Shang city wall found in the center of the modern industrial town of Zhengzhou. Dating from about 1600 B.C., this wall survives for great lengths, and in superb condition. When I climbed up onto it in 1981, I found it towering over the neighboring houses, and so wide on top that their occupants had plowed and planted its fertile mud as a cornfield. Elsewhere in the city the threat that required that wall was dramatically demonstrated: In a ditch were found the skulls of dozens of young men, severed and dumped there after some undocumented slaughter nearly 3,500 years ago.

North of Zhengzhou near the modern town of Anyang, the embattled Shang rulers had their capital for three centuries; and there an unlooted royal tomb was found in 1976. It belonged to Fu Hao, a warrior queen of the 12th century B.C. Chinese annals tell us that she led an army of 13,000 men. Fu Hao's tomb was well stocked with delicate jades, as became an empress, but the most evocative object I saw was the portable kitchen she must have used in the field, with three covered pans for steaming her food, and 3,000-year-old soot still caked on the bottom. While later Chinese rulers accomplished phenomenal feats of construction—with equally phenomenal death rates—such as the Grand Canal and the Great Wall, the pioneering Shang monarchs and their forebears, the shadowy Xia who founded the first Chinese cities, will always hold my greatest interest.

Perhaps this is because in my own research area, in Central America, the ancient Maya were creating a new culture at much the same time. When Fu Hao was leading her troops into battle, the Maya at our little site of Cuello in northern Belize were setting up more peaceful contacts with their neighbors. Brilliant black obsidian and glowing apple-green jade attest to a trade network that linked the tropical forest of Belize with the volcanic highlands of Guatemala 300 miles to the south. On the caravan routes of Asia, strings of camels plodded the miles; horse-drawn and ox-drawn carts rumbled their way between city and city, oasis and oasis, as they traveled the arrow-straight roads of the later Roman Empire; but Maya trade passed silently along jungle trails on human backs.

In all the Americas there were no animals suited to carrying a rider or drawing a vehicle; the wheel was used only for toys. The Maya and their

---

*Alternative solutions to a builder's problem: The corbeled, or false, arch (left)
consists of layers of brick or stone, each projecting farther than the one below. Mere
weight of material, with or without mortar, holds up such a structure. Wedge-shaped
blocks and center keystone give stability to the rounded "Roman" arch (right).
FOLLOWING PAGES: In A.D. 550, at Ctesiphon in modern Iraq, builders of a palace for
Sassanian kings used both for a hall 86 feet wide at the floor. They employed corbeling
in the lower courses of the walls, a true arch in the soaring barrel-vault ceiling.*

neighbors packed their goods into a bag held on the shoulders by a tump-line, a forehead sling that helped to spread the load. Even so, a Maya porter could carry only about forty pounds, about a third of the burden taken by an Asian mule. Many years ago I helped my workmen bring out the excavated pottery from a site deep in the jungle. I bowed my head to the tumpline, and set out on a narrow switchback trail over limestone hills. It was hot; parrots screeched and howler monkeys howled; insects *churred* and buzzed and bit. Within a few miles I began to appreciate the contribution of draft animals to trade and technology, and to think about the difference in resources available to the builders of the ancient civilizations of the Old and New Worlds.

In construction as in transportation, the Native Americans had to rely on human muscle alone. Apparently neither the Maya nor the Inca, two of the most accomplished civilizations, had the pulley or the screw, major energy-saving devices in Eurasian cultures. Although metalworking began early in Peru, and spread north into Mexico by about A.D. 800, it was used first to make jewelry and later for weapons (as it had been in the Old World). Metal tools appear only when both the ore and technology for working it become sufficiently cheap. The Spanish conquistadors interrupted an Inca civilization at the technological level of Bronze Age Europe, and conquered a Maya area equipped for the late Stone Age.

This laggard technology still makes me pause in amazement when I see some of the monuments it produced. Near Mexico City at Teotihuacán, the Pyramid of the Sun, dating from about the time of Christ, has a base the size of that in the Great Pyramid of Egypt; on this base men piled an estimated million cubic yards of fill. The Classic Maya moved far greater volumes of earth digging drainage canals in floodplain country, and greater amounts of limestone rubble for paved roads and causeways. In the high Andes of Peru, Inca workmen were able to move stone blocks weighing 140 tons up and down steep mountainsides. Jean-Pierre Protzen, a professor of architecture at Berkeley, has been able to work out how most Inca stone-moving was done, but pieces of this size defy his imagination. We discussed the problem recently. In theory, 2,400 men could move a 140-ton block—but how could enough rope be secured to it? How could 2,400 men maneuver along a narrow winding road? "How it was done still baffles me," said Jean-Pierre, shrugging his shoulders.

More than 12,000 feet above sea level, on the treeless plateau of Huánuco Pampa, the Incas built a city on the Royal Road that linked Cuzco to their northern capital at Quito. As you approach Huánuco from the north, you see their *qollqa*, or storehouses, standing in serried lines; once they were filled with foodstuffs, textiles, and weapons such as lances and darts. As well as a gathering place for tribute, the city was a strategic arms dump—and a ceremonial center.

When the ruling Inca arrived in state, borne on a golden litter, he

Roofed only by the sky, 134 close-set sandstone columns once supported a painted ceiling—338 by 170 feet—over the great Hypostyle Hall of the Temple of Amun at Karnak. Post-and-lintel construction reduced open space to narrow aisles in this immense chamber, a coronation hall of the Pharaohs in the 13th century B.C.

Tugging on palm-fiber ropes, workmen in 1816 drag a seven-ton head toward the Nile, museum bound. One man eases a log under the platform as it inches forward. Ancient crews used the ropes but not, apparently, the rollers—strong timbers had to be imported, and men were cheap. A mural in a 4,000-year-old tomb shows a colossal statue on a sledge, with a man pouring lubricant

under its runners. From the tomb inscriptions a modern scholar estimated this load at 132 tons and the work gang at about 2,000 men. Probably a drummer set the cadence so they pulled in unison. Egyptian artists portrayed oxen dragging small unworked stone blocks, but only men hauling great statues and ponderous obelisks.

33

would have crossed the Huánuco bridge, which until its destruction by floods in 1980 must have looked much as it did in pre-Hispanic times. It had piers of stone cantilevered out over the fast-flowing Orqomayu, supporting a surface of seven logs more than 50 feet long. Down to it came the Royal Road, with broad steps to ease the descent of men and llamas bringing tribute, drains to take off rainwater, and a wall on the downslope side to keep the highway from collapsing. This spinal route of the Inca Empire ran more than a thousand miles from Quito to Cuzco, and farther south into Chile and Argentina. Even today it gives me a sense of living history whenever I walk on it, and stirs a poignant memory of the great civilization that Pizarro destroyed.

On the north coast of Peru where Inca forces conquered the rival monarchy of Chimor less than a century earlier, I have stood in a desert bleakness that reminds me powerfully of the Mesopotamian plain around Ur. Here is another place where canals brought life to the landscape. The Chimu capital of Chan Chan consists of a sequence of huge *ciudadelas*, walled mud-brick compounds set amid a gaggle of small mud houses.

Monuments to notables long dead, aringa ora, *or "living faces," gaze impassively from the flank of an Easter Island volcano. Workers raise a fallen statue with elementary equipment probably used by their Polynesian forebears: rubble to prop the multi-ton image, a strong pole for a lever, thick rope, and muscle.*

New York architect Bill Conklin has spent many years studying the ancient Peruvian builders, and notes that these compound walls were higher and thicker than any threat, internal or external, could warrant. He sees their function as "the creation of an image of power."

The ancient Peruvians treated the very landscape as something to be modeled into art on a giant scale. Bill Conklin has analyzed the ways in which early ceremonial centers reflect their surroundings, linking the real mountains with man-made mountains of brick. The largest and earliest of these sites, El Paraiso near Lima, held a courtyard that may have extended for 18 acres, and may have been built as early as 2000 B.C. While the conquistadors were rightly impressed by Inca civilization, we can be even more amazed at the achievements of the preceding millennia.

Closer to home, we can be equally taken aback by the ingenuity and application of the ancient North Americans. In West Carroll Parish in Louisiana, just west of the Mississippi, lies Poverty Point. At ground level the site is a series of inconspicuous earthworks, bank after bank enclosing a huge central space bounded by the Bayou Macon. From the air I could see the pattern. Like the multiple earthworks of Maiden Castle, or the *pa* hill-forts of New Zealand's Maori, the six concentric ridges of Poverty Point lie one within the other, 4,000 feet across at their widest. Unlike those fortified sites, this settlement had low ridges, on flat ground. Beyond those arcs stood two sentinel or ceremonial mounds; one, more than 70 feet high, apparently had an artificial access ramp. All these were built up basketload by basketload. Archaeologist James Ford found that the impressions of plaited baskets, one to two feet in diameter, had survived on the stiff local clay. Clarence Webb, M.D., an avocational archaeologist who has worked at Poverty Point for decades, has estimated that 30 million 50-pound basketloads went into the building of Poverty Point.

What is amazing, rather than just impressive, about the site is this: Apparently it was built by people who had not yet developed the art of farming—around 1000 B.C. or even earlier. They were contemporaries of the Olmec of Mexico, who also settled on natural riverside levees, but lacked the Olmec staples of maize and beans. Clarence Webb feels, despite the lack of conclusive evidence, that the size of Poverty Point and the presence of grinding stones imply that crops were grown here as in Mesoamerica. Jon Gibson, who has dug at the site in recent years, differs. He thinks that hunting and gathering at the forest edges in this bountiful region would supply more than enough food. "I'm convinced that a harvesting program, geared to the seasons and coupled with regional distribution, could have produced the communal surplus," he says. The early history of sites such as Jericho bears him out.

On a recent visit I discussed these conundrums with Mitchell Hillman, curator of the Poverty Point state park and museum. He showed me how

Concentric semicircles of earth (vivid in infrared) once embraced the largest North American village of its time: About 1000 B.C., several thousand people may have lived at Louisiana's Poverty Point. The ridges—originally perhaps 15 to 25 feet high, 50 to 150 feet wide, built by the basketload—may have held small houses in well-ordered groups. The outer ridge spans nearly three-quarters of a mile.

so-called bannerstones could be used to weight a pump-drill, creating a flywheel effect for working hard stone, and coached me through a practice session with an atlatl, or spear thrower. While the atlatl increases the range of a spear, Mitchell thinks it was probably more useful in increasing the impact of a hit. Either way, it would have brought in more venison—enough, he suspects, to support major changes in a way of life.

The deepest questions of Poverty Point confront us at the sites of great works all over the world: What kind of society found this structure necessary? How did our ancestors develop the architectural and engineering principles that have left us such a rich heritage? How did they conceive those towering shrines and powerful fortresses in the first place?

The following chapters explore these questions in the context of particular traditions. (Of necessity, they define "antiquity" in different ways. In Europe, "ancient" usually means "before the fall of Rome"; in the new world, "before European conquest." Muslim conquests in India, and alien dynasties in China, mark significant change in cultures centuries old.) Each account reports new findings, of the sort that I have enjoyed in recent years. As I visited with English excavators who are reexamining the hill-forts, listened to the news out of Mohenjo Daro from Michael Jansen, and discussed the superb jades from Fu Hao's tomb with the late Xia Nai, dean of China's archaeologists, one thought kept coming into my mind—and Mitchell Hillman expressed it perfectly, in his pleasant drawl: "At last we're starting to get some answers out of all this mess."

37

GREECE AND ROME

GREECE AND ROME

By Gene S. Stuart
Photographs by Blaine Harrington III

I n the light of a crystalline Greek morning, early in May, acanthus leaves as dark as winter shadows curled against their milky likenesses carved in marble two thousand years ago. Those sculpted leaves identified a block of stone as the capital, or crowning member, of a column in the style called Corinthian but developed in Athens. Some later violence, natural or human, had hurled the block to the ground. Now it lay on golden sand at my feet and breezes set the living thistle leaves swaying against the marble motif. Present and past echoed in chorus; art complemented life; life reconfirmed a sculpted timelessness.

On that day in Athens, the Agora—the ancient public square—seemed a quiet, aged garden. Trees and shrubs grew interspersed with remains of civic buildings and temples. Rows of broken columns, slumping courses of walls, gleaming steps, and fallen pediments lay among walkways and thoroughfares. Here men had strolled in the sun, or in the shade of the roofed colonnades called stoas, to discuss a promising athlete or playwright, to gossip, to argue about local politics or foreign alliances. Here they gathered as jurors, or elected public officials, or shopped for goods as varied as turnips and fine bronzes. The ruins of structures sprawled juxtaposed upon traces of older structures, just as cultures build on cultures. I had come to Athens to find Greek roots of the classical civilization that Rome bequeathed to the world we now call Western.

In his office in the reconstructed Stoa of Attalos, archaeologist John Camp of the American School of Classical Studies took time to discuss this theme. "Romans," he said, "were impressed with most things Greek."

Not least of the things they admired was architecture, and in Athens this reached its zenith in the fourth and fifth centuries B.C. John and I talked about the famed Greek orders of style: the acanthus-leafed Corinthian, the scrolled Ionic, the plain Doric. "Athenian architecture was more austere than that of much of the Greek world and more under the influence of Doric," John said in summary.

On the sacred Acropolis, the great pink-tinted stone hill looming above us, stood the most famed of all Doric temples, the golden-hued Parthenon, its columns unadorned except for fluting. I was to climb the hill repeatedly and at various times of day, to sit on a column drum or a weathered block and study the subtle and severe elegance of the building, the changing aspect brought by the play of light.

Its construction began in 447 B.C., part of a rebuilding program that fol-

PRECEDING PAGES: Serviceable even today, a Roman road meanders through Syria. Beginning in the third century B.C., legionaries built highways while marching to conquest, constructing causeways, tunnels, and bridges as terrain required. Completed under the Empire, the network linked the classical world.

N.G.S. PHOTOGRAPHER JAMES L. STANFIELD

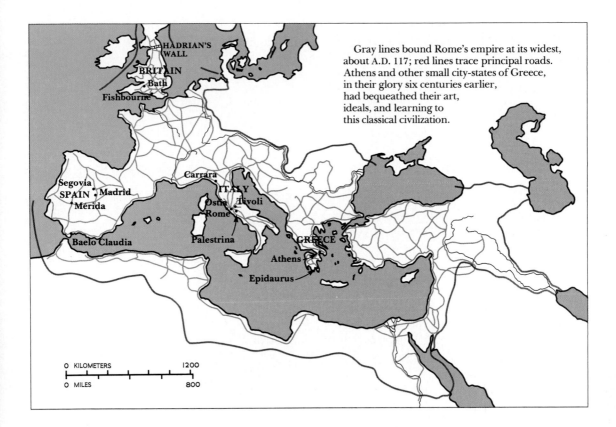

Gray lines bound Rome's empire at its widest, about A.D. 117; red lines trace principal roads. Athens and other small city-states of Greece, in their glory six centuries earlier, had bequeathed their art, ideals, and learning to this classical civilization.

lowed a brief but disastrous Persian invasion. The Parthenon, or Temple of the Maiden, would honor Athena, virgin goddess of war and wisdom, protectress of Athens. The great general and statesman Pericles engaged distinguished architects, Iktinos and Callicrates, to design the new temple and the master sculptor Phidias to supervise construction. A multitude of workmen and technicians quarried the prized Pentelic marble from a nearby mountain and labored mightily to transport roughed-out blocks and drums to the Acropolis, hoist them into place, and finish the fine details. Enclosed in a small inner shrine stood Phidias' gold-and-ivory statue of the goddess. In 438 came the dedication.

Centuries before, Greek architects had built rectangular temples of wood with simple post-and-lintel construction. By the fifth century B.C. deforestation had made suitable trees all but impossible to find nearby. Easily carved substitutes such as limestone became popular, but builders of the classic period preferred the noblest of stones, marble. Even though architects knew of arches and vaults as forms suited to masonry, they usually built as if they were still using wood. Wooden beams could span a gap of 50 feet or less; builders spanned the same distances with a stone entablature (the horizontal structure of architrave, frieze, and cornice, between the columns and the pediment or the roof).

Moreover, the small Greek city-states lacked the labor reserves of Egypt or eastern empires, and free citizens could not be forced into work gangs at a ruler's whim. After about 515 B.C., Greek builders employed stone in blocks of ten tons or less, which could be raised (Continued on page 47)

41

Restored to the standards of Greece in the fourth century B.C., the theater at Epidaurus displays its builders' ingenious use of natural slopes. Here as many as 14,000 spectators enjoyed good sight lines and perfect acoustics for performances of drama, music, and poetry. The site honored Asklepios, god of healing, whose priests interpreted health-giving dreams. Drama laid bare the

human mind and soul, an integral part of curing ritual. In a Greek city-state, the theater could hold all citizens in assembly. With so small a labor force, sixth-century builders stopped using ramps to raise their stones and relied on a new device: a crane run by pulleys and winches. In the theater, the crane let a "god" or "goddess" descend to the stage as if from heaven.

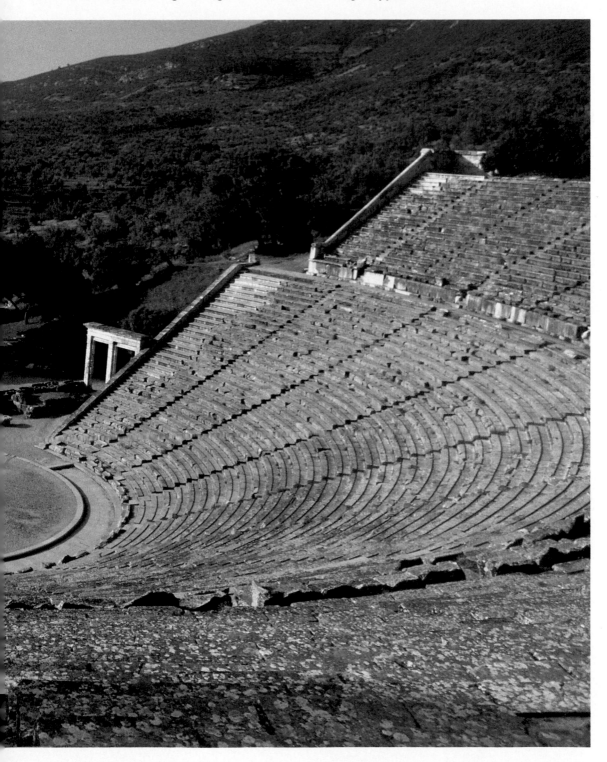

by a crane with pulleys and man-powered winches. Barbarians might take pride in using huge stones for enormous structures, but Greeks—especially Athenians—were content to work within reasonable limits, seeking beauty in perfected form. Temple proportions gained refinement, and the supreme example is the Parthenon. (Its columns look absolutely straight because they are ever so slightly convex: by eleven-sixteenths of an inch in a height of 31 feet.) Still, the basic temple plan remained almost unchanged, as did some details of construction.

I found some of these details on the facade of the Parthenon, where I saw six *guttae* (literally, in Latin, drops of liquid) carved at regular intervals. They represent wooden pegs driven into the ends of wooden beams. Elements of the frieze take the shape of older prototypes that shielded wooden beams from damaging wind and rain. But the interior of the temple makes little provision for sheltering assembled worshipers. Exterior space was far more important.

"Greek liturgy and public ceremony generally took place outside a building," John Camp had remarked. "There was no need to go inside except to see the cult statue."

By the sixth century B.C. Greek structures shone in the Mediterranean sunlight like beacons to the less accomplished Romans. Rome had developed little beyond a collection of roundish wattle-and-daub huts sprawled on a hill. Yet as it grew and increased in power, Rome began to borrow Greek ideas, and attracted or captured many educated and talented Greeks. Eventually, Athens allied herself with an enemy of Rome, and after a long siege the Roman general Sulla captured and looted the city. His plunder included unpublished works by Aristotle.

"Sulla sent a column capital back to Rome," remarked John Camp. "The architect had been a Roman working in Athens. It comes full cycle." Rome enforced her own rule thereafter, and put up buildings, but the Athenians maintained their language and much of their tradition. As John reminded me, "Athens was the center of Mediterranean culture and education, and never gave up that role."

In Italy, Rome had developed robust architectural styles of its own making. Twenty-four miles south and east of the capital lies Palestrina, a settlement already well established by 753 B.C., Rome's legendary year of founding. Spilling down the slopes of Monte Ginestro, it was a place favored by gods and coveted by humans, where an oracle mouthed divine revelations. Romans captured and destroyed the center, and about 80 B.C. rebuilt it into a superb monument of the Republican era—a sanctuary dedicated to Fortuna Primigenia, the Goddess of Fortune, firstborn daughter of Jupiter the supreme god.

Timeless temple to Athena, the Parthenon crowns Athenian achievement. Distinguished architects calculated its subtle proportions; craftsmen expressed perfection of Doric style. It withstood earthquakes only to fall in A.D. 1687— used by Turkish rulers to store gunpowder, it suffered a wartime explosion. PRECEDING PAGES: *Evzones—elite infantry—march from the Propylaea, gateway to the Acropolis. Its unusually wide span, a triumph of ancient construction, gave passage to solemn yearly processions honoring the city's patron goddess.*

Sulla may have commissioned the project. An unknown Roman architect used a central axis and seven terraces in a broadly pyramidal scheme. He combined an interplay of ramps, niches, vaults, arcades, open spaces and enclosed rooms. He emphasized half-circular forms called hemicycles, and a great semicircular arcade dominates the upper zone. In this, say Italian scholars, "Roman architecture has its real beginning."

Near the foot of the mountain I met Pietro Giuseppe Tomassi, or Peppino, a seventh-generation native of Palestrina and, appropriately, a builder. As we climbed the slippery cobbled streets of the town and the ascending terraces of the sanctuary, he pointed out those ancient building techniques that had expressed an era's new freedom of design.

"For the most part it was the use of mortared stone and concrete," Peppino commented. "And they were beginning to do what they wanted with new form. Now, the most sacred part was here in the lower part—the Lower Sanctuary." He indicated a little dark recess. "There they kept tablets to interpret the oracle's proclamations." Locals still refer to it with awe as the Antro delle Sorti, the Cave of Destinies.

Roman pilgrims came by the thousand, perhaps to witness long-forgotten ritual, surely to marvel and pray. We paused at a colonnade with coffered vaulting—vaulting with recessed panels. "Here were small shops for religious souvenirs," said Peppino. Supplicants bought small terra-cotta figurines of the goddess to take away and cherish—a custom that survives, with Christian images, from Italy to Latin America.

At the end of the fourth century A.D. a Christian emperor closed Palestrina's pagan complex. Sanctuary was reduced to shelter; elegant colonnades became stables. In time, a medieval town obliterated the terraced sanctuary, growing into an unplanned jumble of houses.

Peppino and I reached the uppermost hemicycle. Above this the statue of Fortuna had stood, in a small circular temple. Today the curving steps are crowned by the concave facade of a medieval palace, now the sanctuary museum. We looked down past the terraces to the modern structures at the foot of the mountain. A line of dark trees edged the Via Praenestina, the ancient road to Rome; a cluster of dark trees marked one of the Emperor Hadrian's summer villas. Beyond, mountains faded into distant haze rather than horizon.

"I remember that January 8, 1944, was so clear you could see Anzio there on the coast 25 miles ahead, and American ships in the harbor," said Peppino. With a start I remembered the Anzio beachhead, one of the desperate battles of World War II. "That's the day American planes first came and the bombing began." The final raids came on May 22, as more than 500 B17s and B24s hit Palestrina. When the dust of destruction settled, centuries of construction had been blasted away and the great Roman sanctuary once again looked out toward the sea. "We have the Americans to thank for that good fortune," laughed Peppino.

I took the ancient road back to Rome, pausing often to look back. A warm drizzle began. On a section of the road's original basalt paving stones, I stopped the car beneath a sheltering tree. I dined on fruit, bread, and cheese, and rested, as other pilgrims must have done before me.

At the height of empire, in the first and second centuries A.D., all roads indeed led to Rome. A dozen major highways paved with stone radiated like spokes from that hub of power. In theory they began and ended at a golden milestone in the Forum, that teeming civic and religious heart of the capital, a place of exquisite sculpture, awesome monuments, and magnificent buildings; a place where leaders determined the fate of tribes and nations as easily as they honored heroes and gods. By then Rome was so famed that people referred to it simply as *Urbs*—the City.

Such roads had been constructed primarily for military use, helping speed Rome from Republic to Empire. Legionaries themselves built many roads, marching out with picks and shovels and axes. Construction techniques varied according to local terrain and materials. In soggy lowlands a wooden corduroy base, or close-set pilings, served as foundations; on better ground, ditches drained the roadway. Paving might consist of gravel in thin mortar, cobblestones set in clay, or large stone slabs. Terrain permitting, level shoulders flanked the paving, and scholars think that wheeled traffic normally used these surfaces.

Legions and government officials had priority of use, but roads also hurried merchants, artisans, and scholars to far-flung provinces. Bounds of empire ran from the Euphrates River in the east to Britain, from the Danube River in the north to the Sahara. Along the frontiers, roads often dwindled into trails or led to trade routes. Quite a few Romans ventured into Black Africa, legendary land of exotic beasts; there were tales of another great empire, China, source of that enigmatic luxury, silk.

Sea routes crisscrossed the Mediterranean and skirted farther coasts of Europe, Africa, and Asia. But even Rome had her limits, in the great stream of ocean that surrounded the known world.

She had acquired distant territories long before, but it was Augustus Caesar, successor to Julius Caesar, who brought grandeur to the world's most powerful city. His rule, from 27 B.C. to A.D. 14, marked the end of civil wars and the beginning of the *Pax Romana*, the Roman Peace that would continue through many reigns.

Earlier builders had relied on local materials—wood and tiles, brick, the limestone called travertine and the porous dull-colored tufa, a compacted volcanic dust. Only occasionally did they add facings and flourishes of marble imported from Greece, Africa, or Asia Minor. Augustus utilized marble quarries at Carrara, more than 230 miles to the north, and boasted with some justice that he "found Rome a city of brick and left it a city of marble." His program included a new Forum, temples, baths, and theaters. In addition, his son-in-law Agrippa took charge of building walls and gates, renovating the city's drainage system, enlarging four aqueducts and adding two more. These doubled Rome's water supply.

Eventually the city population numbered *(Continued on page 54)*

FOLLOWING PAGES: Rome's distinctive blend of practical engineering, imposing scale, and daunting splendor lives on in the Colosseum, most famed of her amphitheaters. Wooden floors—spread with sand (arena) to absorb spilled blood—once covered this maze of structures that held machinery, cages of wild beasts, and humans doomed to combat and death before 50,000 spectators.

Cloud-high quarry in the Apuan Alps near Carrara, Italy, yields one of the world's most famous marbles, which brought splendor to imperial Rome. Motor-powered cables cut the stone today, aided by one of man's first abrasives: sand. The ancient quarries lay at much lower elevations. There workmen split the rock with specialized iron pickaxes: a method used until recently. In living memory, wooden sleds controlled—more or less—by strong men with wire cables eased the blocks downhill. Roman oxcarts hauled the stone to the port town, Luna, for shipment south to the capital. Builders and sculptors used it lavishly; medieval artisans reused it. Quarrying revived in the Renaissance; the great sculptor Michelangelo chose Carrara marble for masterpieces inspired by classical statuary. Today sculptors from many lands live in and near Carrara. At left, Aitor de Mendizabal, a young Basque from Spain, chisels a work in progress; he strives to bring the power of ancient Roman portraiture to sculpture in the living style of the present day.

something between half a million and a million, including many slaves. The privileged few had the luxury of a city mansion and country villa, but many lived in crowded boardinghouses, apartments of variable quality, or grim tenements. The Greek geographer Strabo, who settled in Rome about 29 B.C., noted the turmoil of construction: "They built incessantly because of the collapses and fires and repeated sales. . . ." Graft and shoddy practices had come into play even earlier. The Republic's great orator Cicero had complained: "Two of my shops have fallen down and the rest are cracking: not only have the tenants fled but even the mice have migrated."

While Greek craftsmen came to cut and carve the Augustan marble, Roman architecture had its own distinctive forms: basilicas, amphitheaters, and public baths. A civic building, the basilica was a large rectangu-

Massive vaults frame visitors to the Large Baths at Hadrian's Villa. Stripped of marble facings, the baths show building techniques. Concrete-vault roofs allow spacious rooms. A thick concrete core gives strength to unrestored walls, still holding their original alternating courses of brick and tufa. The emperor, himself an architect, ordered copies of Athens' famed caryatids (weight-bearing statues) to adorn a garden pool; one of them graces the building used as a museum at the Villa today.

lar hall for public business and the administration of justice. Christians in later centuries would adapt the basilica for religious services.

Amphitheaters provided seating for multitudes eager to enjoy the spectacles that emperors felt obligated to provide (circuses, said the satirist Juvenal, and bread kept the populace satisfied). Both setting and entertainment differed significantly from Greek counterparts. The Greek theater would take advantage of a hillside slope; and while comedy allowed outspoken vulgarity, tragedy kept episodes of violence offstage. The typical Roman amphitheater was a freestanding structure; and its spectacles included gladiators fighting each other, or wild animals, to the death. Victims ranged from aggressive bears and lions to bewildered ostriches and giraffes; from slave swordsmen to Christian martyrs.

Largest of these enclosures was the Colosseum, built between A.D. 70

and 80 with a seating capacity of perhaps 50,000 or more. Its immense size—an ellipse 620 by 513 feet externally—was new; its form and construction had Republican precedents. Concrete foundations 40 feet deep assured stability; travertine masonry supported the heaviest load, and a travertine facade covered structural brick. On the facade, each of the three stories contained 80 arches framed by engaged columns: Doric at ground level, Ionic above that, Corinthian next. Above these rose an attic story with Corinthian pilasters and stone brackets. The brackets held poles that supported a great awning, manipulated with ropes by a detachment of sailors.

Inside, an ingenious system of stairways and corridors, entrances and exits, provided for crowd control. The sectioned wooden floor concealed a service area for essentials such as armor, animal cages, and counterweighted hoists. Usually the floor was covered with *arena,* or sand, but on occasion the central area was flooded for mock naval battles.

For day-to-day pleasures, the distinctively Roman facilities were *thermae,* or public baths. Here people met to steam, soak, swim, gossip, read, or make business deals. Murals, mosaics, and stucco adornments, fountains and statues, gave the masses a sense of sharing imperial splendor. The largest thermae could accommodate thousands of visitors at once. Those completed by Caracalla in A.D. 216, including their gardens, covered nearly four times the area of the Acropolis in Athens, and one gargantuan room now serves as a stage for productions of opera in summer.

Baths, flooded amphitheaters, fountains—the demand for water increased until Rome's became the largest public water-supply system in the ancient world. Frontinus, a water commissioner during the first century A.D., wrote proudly: "Will anybody compare the Pyramids, or those . . . useless though renowned works of the Greeks, with these aqueducts, with these many indispensable structures?"

In one of the most famous of ancient disasters, Rome went up in flames in July of A.D. 64—while, supposedly, the emperor Nero played the fiddle. (He did not; violins developed from medieval instruments.) Suetonius, gossipy biographer of the Caesars, reported that Nero watched "enraptured by what he called 'the beauty of the flames'; then put on his tragedian's costume and sang *The Fall of Ilium* from beginning to end."

Rumor had it that Nero himself had arranged for the fire, which left only four of the city's fourteen sections intact. Better authority, the historian Tacitus, reports that he ordered the city rebuilt with new safeguards. All structures were to be of fire-resistant stone, and without common walls; separated by "broad thoroughfares" and other open spaces. A modern scholar, architectural historian William L. MacDonald, points out that the new materials could be prepared as standard units, and, he says,

Unprecedented marvel, the Pantheon survives as proof of Roman genius. Builders put 5,000 tons of concrete over wooden forms to shape the dome; its coffers (recessed panels) lighten the enormous load while rounded vaults distribute it among eight piers, the sole supporting members. Built by the Emperor Hadrian, this unique temple honors "all the gods"; the dome, largest of antiquity, suggests the sphere of heaven. Michelangelo called it "an angelic, not a human, design."

"a rich strain of creativity pervaded this rational structure of events."

Nero's power, riches, and devotion to the arts gave architecture new impetus and architects new freedom. The fire had destroyed a palace he had just begun. With two skilled engineers, Severus and Celer, as architects, he put up a new one, the *Domus Aurea,* or Golden House. Nothing so grandiose had been seen before—"True gentlemen always throw their money about," Nero liked to say—and nothing so innovative.

He took more than 300 acres for its setting, so that an artificial lake and landscaped plantings of fields, vineyards, and trees could suggest a country villa in the heart of the city. The palace had a triple portico a mile long, and a vestibule large enough to house a statue of Nero 120 feet tall. Suetonius reported: "In the rest of the palace all parts were overlaid with gold and adorned with gems and mother-of-pearl. There were dining rooms with fretted ceilings of ivory, whose panels could turn and shower down flowers and were fitted with pipes for sprinkling the guests with perfumes. The main banquet hall was circular and constantly revolved day and night, like the heavens." When these sumptuous interiors were ready, said Suetonius, the emperor "condescended to remark, 'Good, now I can at last begin to live like a human being!'"

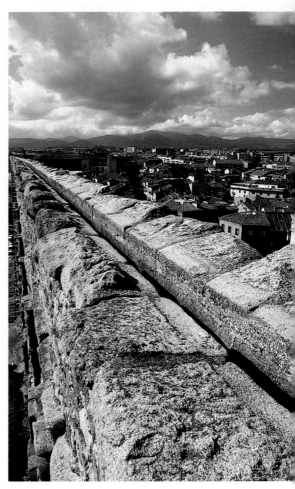

Grand in concept and practical in scheme, the aqueduct of Segovia, Spain, holds a constant gradient as it crosses a valley 90 feet below on two tiers of arches. Skill, not mortar, joins ton upon ton of granite blocks, many of them drilled for iron pegs to facilitate transportation and to anchor scaffolding. After 17 centuries the system still functions. It speeds mountain spring water from ten miles away through the conduit (right) into the city. In 312 B.C. Roman officials began their Republic's first aqueduct. Engineers soon improved the design of channels, piping, and supporting structures. As they extended new aqueducts across the miles, they acquired their mastery of the arch. And in time the freestanding arch became, appropriately enough, the symbol of Roman triumph.

Only one wing has survived, and that underground—the Emperor Trajan utilized it as foundations for public baths on the Esquiline Hill. On a bright summer day, architect Pio Baldi of Rome's Istituto Centrale del Restauro handed me a flashlight, and we entered a labyrinth as cold as a natural cavern. For more than an hour I followed Pio along high-vaulted corridors, across polygonal rooms, through doorway after doorway. Finally we came to an octagonal room flooded with light from an *oculus,* a circular opening in the domed concrete ceiling.

An adjoining room housed a concrete incline, and Pio believes that a waterfall cascaded down it. "It's often thought that this was the banquet hall described by Suetonius," he said. "And that the dome didn't revolve, but that a circular wooden floor moved, powered by water flowing underneath it." Powered, in effect, like a Roman water mill.

Recent excavations disprove this much-disputed theory, while scholars agree on the importance of the palace. It introduced a revolutionary new style. William MacDonald says: "Roofed by high concave surfaces, these new interiors expressed an architectonic vitality unknown in the static world of flat-roofed rooms of rectangular plan." The English archaeologist J. B. Ward-Perkins thought it "hardly an exaggeration to say that the

59

Luxury serves the Roman public in a re-creation of the Baths of Diocletian. In the foreground, men savor the warmth of the tepidarium; *beyond the arch, the* frigidarium *offers a cold plunge, a bracing contrast to the hot* caldarium *nearby. At fixed hours women enjoy exclusive*

PAINTING BY ALAN SORRELL. FROM *GREECE AND ROME — THE BIRTH OF CIVILIZATION*. PUBLISHED BY THAMES AND HUDSON, LONDON

*use of all these rooms. Children enter free, and the emperor may buy popularity by assuming
the token charge for adults. Mosaics and marble veneers lend splendor to the concrete vaults,
Rome's most innovative structures—seen here on the most grandiose scale.*

whole subsequent history of European architectural thought hangs upon this historic event. . . ."

The key to this was Roman concrete: developed by trial and error through three centuries from mediocre mortar to artificial stone.

"It was an enormous contribution," architect-archaeologist Dr. Eugenia Salza Prina Ricotti told me. "A revolution comparable to the one brought about by steel-and-concrete techniques in modern times." The Romans employed *pozzolana*, a finely ground volcanic sand, with lime and water and aggregate (often tufa), and the resulting mixture was strong, waterproof, and fire-resistant. "I have found it worked well in stress," said Dr. Ricotti. "They could form shapes—large vaults, domes." She smiled broadly. "It was new—and Roman building really begins to be splendid with Emperor Hadrian, who was an architect himself."

Architect, painter, poet, mathematician, and more, Hadrian was by nature restless, quick, and curious. A later writer said that he applied his administrative genius to the arts: "He enrolled by cohorts and centuries, on the model of the legions, builders, geometers, architects, and every sort of expert in construction or decoration." William MacDonald says: "He asked for buildings continually, collecting them as other men collected sculpture or gems."

Perhaps Hadrian's finest gem, certainly the best preserved, is the Pantheon, in Rome. Behind the columns and pediment of a traditional Roman temple facade he constructed a circular, domed hall of brick-faced concrete. Eight piers support a concrete dome decorated with coffers that diminish in size and depth as they rise. The chamber's width and height are the same, 150 Roman feet; the oculus is 30 Roman feet in diameter.

MacDonald pictures the building in progress: "Armies of workmen,

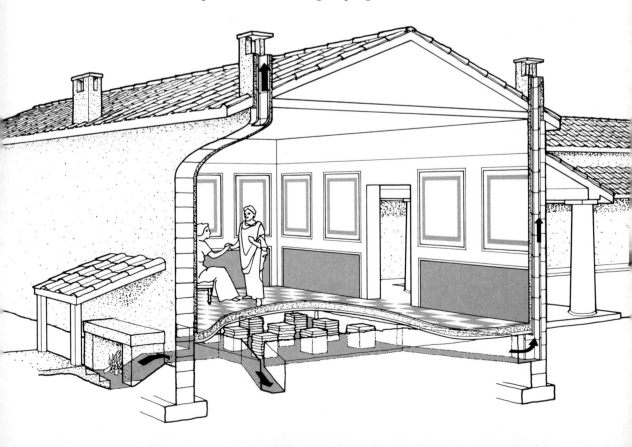

scheduled according to the drying time of the mortar, swarmed along the exterior scaffolding, and up and down the ladders and ramps, while others operated the multi-pulleyed cranes.... As the concrete dried, the marble fitters, bronze workers, and other specialists occupied the inner woodwork, finishing and decorating the interior surfaces." As the dome rose, the mix of concrete varied, with heavy aggregate at the bottom and porous lightweight pumice mixed in toward the top. The ancient engineers employed sound methods, he says; "the five thousand-odd tons of concrete that form the dome are still in place."

The Pantheon, Temple of All the Gods, hailed Hadrian's Greco-Roman heritage and symbolized the unity of the ancient world under imperial power. It celebrated traditional religion, but expressed a new fascination with a kind of science and with the cosmos.

Near Tivoli, on a plain overlooked by mountains and nourished by rushing streams, Hadrian built his ideal residence, a villa with all the resources of an imperial town. Dr. Ricotti has been excavating at the site for 16 years. "I'm working on it yet," she commented as she explained a map that shows some 500 acres. We examined the plan of a subway system for vehicles that ran for a total of two miles underground. She pointed out underground depositories that she thinks were used for storing snow: "They used it for refrigerating food, making cold drinks and cold dishes—an ancestor of gazpacho, a kind of salad soup, for example. This villa was a place where an emperor could stay and rule all the world under him without being disturbed too much by the Senate." She laughed, then added a serious summary: "Rome and the world came to him."

Visitors still come. To stroll these ruins is to enter an emperor's magical dream, and I spent hours in amazement and in reverie.

Central heating Roman style, a major development from the first century A.D., made the villa as livable in northern provinces as in a Mediterranean climate. Hot air from a furnace circulates among piers beneath the floor, then rises through tile flues to warm the walls. The example at right survived at Fishbourne, in southern England. The system's name, hypocaust, comes from a Latinized Greek word meaning "room heated from below." Installed on a grand scale in public baths, the hypocaustum *inspired dramatic progress in plumbing—another practical art in which Romans excelled.*
FOLLOWING PAGES: *Sacred thermal springs at Aquae Sulis (now Bath, England) provided natural warmth for a popular bath-and-temple complex. A Victorian structure rises from the Roman ruins; gas flares simulate the torches of antiquity.*

Hadrian's biographer, Aelius Spartianus, wrote: "He built public buildings in all places and without number. . . ." Devoted to Athens, Hadrian built a large library near the Agora. Born in Spain, he decorated Spanish provinces with structures befitting a great ruler's homeland. In Mérida, I admired rare colored marble that he may have donated for the theater. But I found clues to the wealth of the province elsewhere.

Along Spain's south coast where Europe and Africa almost meet, nature sends great schools of tuna through the Strait of Gibraltar. A chain of factories developed to process the catch, and one, Baelo Claudia, became a Roman town. It is now being excavated by a team of French archaeologists. It tells the story of an industry, and illuminates an empire.

Baelo was at the geographic center of this region," project leader Michel Ponsich explained. "We calculate that they prepared at least a thousand cubic meters of salted fish here each month [perhaps 900 tons]. We've found that a cubic meter of fish needs a cubic meter of salt, so there was a salt industry with evaporation ponds. For export, the only containers were amphoras, jars—another industry. There remained the fish waste. They made it into paste, *garum,* a kind of sauce with a thousand uses: as food, mixed with wine, water, or oil, or animal medicine." The best garum was a great luxury. "The riches of these towns!"

Archaeologist Pierre Jacob gave me a tour. There was the road: "Don't imagine a well-paved road like the Via Appia. Rather, a little stone path for mules, donkeys, and pedestrians." The town gate and wall, built about A.D. 50: heavy slathers of mortars on rough stones. "Perhaps when there were no fish running, the fishermen helped build it." Not the walls but the legions were the defenders of a city; walls were symbolic, like Roman art and architecture in general. "To show people: 'Here you are protected, here you are in security. The power of Rome is here.'" We visited the theater, near the far edge of a site of nearly 30 acres. "Big theater for such a little city," said Pierre. "But they had to entertain those hundreds of fishermen, to prevent riots when the sea was rough. I can imagine theater wasn't the most refined here—old Roman peasant humor, very crass."

I found provincial refinement raised to splendor in Britain, at a site called Fishbourne. In A.D. 75, among a native population that lived in circular huts, designers and artisans completed an enormous Roman structure of four wings with painted walls, colorful mosaic floors, colonnades, courtyards, and a suite of baths—the normal luxuries of the elite.

"They uprooted Italy and planted it here," said archaeologist David Rudkin. "It's palatial in scope and in plan as well, with an audience chamber. It's totally out on a limb, an oddity, the sort of thing you associate with a Mediterranean climate. Marvelous there, but absolutely dismal for West Sussex in the winter. What on earth is it doing here?

"Likely it was built for a man named Tiberius Claudius Cogidubnus, who was probably a member of the local tribe's ruling household, taken off to Rome to be educated, and installed here as a client king. It's a fairly common imperial practice—put your own man in at the top to keep the tribes in order." Not far away, Romans rebuilt a round wooden Celtic temple in stone. "It looks like they're saying, 'Well, look, you lads

have been good, you haven't rebelled. Here's a golden handshake.' "

Britain remained part of the Roman Empire for about 360 years, a little longer than the time between the death of Elizabeth I and the accession of Elizabeth II. Roman villas brightened the countryside; Roman roads laid an uneven grid of authority over England; Roman towns brought a network of urban architecture. At hot springs sacred to a local deity, Sulis, Roman engineers tamed the flow to fill a lead-lined stone block reservoir for the thermae of a town now known as Bath. Here a weary traveler from the capital might find the luxury of home in cold and distant isles.

When Hadrian came to power in A.D. 117, he chose to consolidate imperial boundaries rather than to expand them. He ordered a wall built across northern Britain, not a mere military barrier, but rather a visual statement: The power of Rome is here. Starting at the east coast, his legionaries built for 45 miles in stone, the last 31 miles in cut turf. Later they straightened the turf portion, losing about a mile in the process, and replaced the sod with stone. They quarried more than a million cubic yards of it, and built not only a rampart but also 16 large forts and many small turrets. These, with a fortified stone gate every thousand paces (*mille passuum*, the Roman mile of 4,860 feet), sheltered the troops and controlled the movement of traders north into Scotland and back again.

Roughly halfway along the wall at the fort called Housesteads, once garrisoned with 1,000 infantry, I climbed atop the wall to walk westward to the nearest "milecastle." The wall undulates across rolling hills and passes through a shadowy copse. There was no sound except the moan of a cold June wind across the moors and the call of raucous jackdaws.

By A.D. 410, with vital frontiers in Europe insecure, Roman legions had been withdrawn from Britain. Omens of danger had appeared long before, with barbarian invasions from the north. Peacetime commerce did not meet the expense of empire as conquest had done. Moorish pirates attacked Baelo Claudia about A.D. 250, after the little town had enjoyed 200 years of the Roman Peace. Germanic warriors invaded Athens in 267, and once again rubble lay scattered in the Agora: carved column drums, Corinthian capitals, cornices and statues, all in fine marble. Another raid was likely, and the Athenians built a wall.

They constructed it carefully, reshaping their elegant rubble for defense, fitting piece upon piece in dry-stone masonry. They built it well; remnants of one section still stand near Hadrian's library, a noble barricade cool to the touch and glittering in the sun. My conversation with John Camp had ended as he spoke of it: "They were defending Rome's university city." We fell into silence, reflecting on that sad stone testament to the decline of a glorious era and its implication of imminent change. In the eastern lands the Roman Empire would endure for a thousand years; in the west, men faced an age of walls built for necessity, when the power of Rome was gone.

FOLLOWING PAGES: Hadrian's Wall commands high ground on snow-dusted moors of northern England. Built by three Roman legions, the wall defined the northern boundary of Britain. Eventually, barbarians overran such imperial frontiers—to build, in time, a new civilization from the legacy of the old.

ADAM WOOLFITT

MESOAMERICA

MESOAMERICA

By Norman Hammond
Photographs by Steve McCurry

I n the brilliant moonlight of a tropical night at Eastertide I sat in the Great Plaza of Tikal, the largest Classic Maya ruin in Guatemala. It was my first visit. The pale walls of the towering pyramids echoed the noises of the jungle around: a constant racket of howler monkeys, an occasional gruff sound that could have been a jaguar. Then, slowly, it all stopped. The moon dimmed, and the animals went into suspenseful stillness. Nobody had told me there would be a total eclipse of the moon that night, and I sat entranced while in my mind's eye the ghosts of the ancient Maya passed to and fro between the temples.

As the shadow of the world passed from the face of the moon, light returned, and with it the familiar noises of the forest. Once again I could see the buildings around one of the most impressive sacred spaces in the Maya world, the core of the ruined city of the god-kings of the seventh century A.D. At the east and west ends of a plaza the size of a football field rose two massive funerary pyramids. Beneath that on the east, excavators had found the tomb of a man called Ah Cacau, ruler of Tikal in A.D. 700, richly stocked with jade. With him were carved bones bearing his name in Maya hieroglyphics. At the west end rose a second temple, less elegant in its lines, more squat and powerful in feeling. Specialists from the University of Pennsylvania were restoring its exterior, but had never found a tomb in it. To the north of the open space where I sat, smaller temples, with the tombs of Ah Cacau's ancestors, formed a crowded cluster on the North Acropolis. To the south, a complex of courtyards and so-called palaces lay flat and bulky in the shadows; this is thought to have been the residence of the rulers of Tikal. The whole array, in sharp whites and deep shadows, spoke silently of royal power.

At dawn next morning I climbed Temple I, Ah Cacau's monument to himself, ascending the nine-tiered pyramid. Inside the temple, more than a hundred feet above the plaza floor, I examined richly carved lintels. On one the ruler sits enthroned, wearing his regalia of jade jewelry and a towering feathered headdress, beneath the protecting paw of a giant jaguar. On the lintel in Temple II across the plaza, the dominant figure is a woman, perhaps Ah Cacau's consort.

Immense as these buildings are, they reveal more than muscle power: They reveal a vision of the cosmos as the Maya understood it. Jorge Guillemin, the Swiss-born archaeologist who was directing the restoration at the time, explained the pattern to me. The Great Plaza is the most

---

PRECEDING PAGES: Sunlight burnishes structures at Uxmal, highlighting skills of Maya architects. A steep pyramid supports a temple; multi-room buildings range across man-made platforms. Cultures of master builders ruled by demanding elites and dominated by nature deities developed in Mesoamerica around 1200 B.C.

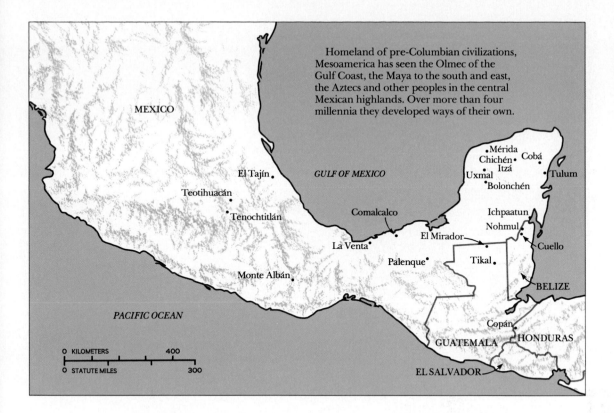

Homeland of pre-Columbian civilizations, Mesoamerica has seen the Olmec of the Gulf Coast, the Maya to the south and east, the Aztecs and other peoples in the central Mexican highlands. Over more than four millennia they developed ways of their own.

grandiose example of a "twin-pyramid group"; seven other such groups are scattered around Tikal, erected by rulers in the seventh and eighth centuries to mark the ends of successive 20-year *katunob,* or sacred periods. We walked through the forest to one of the latest, dedicated in A.D. 771 and now known as Complex Q, and climbed a modest flat-topped pyramid. Looking west into the central plaza, we could see the matching pyramid on the far side, with the vast artificial terrace of the complex dropping away behind it. The twin pyramids mark the rising and setting of the sun. To our right, on the north side of the plaza, we saw a small roofless enclosure containing an upright carved stela with an altar in front of it. On the south lay a long narrow building with nine doorways that open onto a single room. Clemency Coggins and Christopher Jones, then working at Tikal, have shown that the stela represents the sun at noon— thus identifying the ruler with the sun in splendor—while the nine-doored building stands for the underworld with its nine tutelary deities, the Nine Lords of the Night. Thus the circular journey of the sun—rising, zenith, setting, passing below the earth to rise again—is traced on the flat surface of the ground; and by this cosmic diagram the Maya commemorated both the completion of each *katun* and the glory of their rulers.

These twin-pyramid cosmograms come late in the history of Classic Maya civilization, and even later in the development of public architecture in the region we call Mesoamerica. (It covers, roughly, the southern half of Mexico and the adjacent countries of Belize, Guatemala, Honduras, and El Salvador.) More than a thousand years earlier one of the New World's first "pyramids" was built on an island in the coastal swamps by

the Gulf of Mexico: La Venta, constructed by the mysterious "Olmec" who had created a society on the brink of civilization by 1000 B.C. When I visited the site, I found that their pyramid was not a multi-tiered platform like those in Tikal. Nor was it a flat-faced geometric solid, like the Egyptian pyramids which are two millennia older. Looking at this hundred-foot-high mound from a dirt road, I thought it resembled nothing so much as a giant Jell-O mold, although some experts think that its fluted-cone shape copies a volcanic ash heap, or even a volcano itself.

This pyramid has never been excavated, but a magnetometer survey hinted that a stone chamber might lie at its heart. If so, the stone must have been imported, like that used for the giant sculptured heads which are the site's best-known monuments. These, probably portraits of the rulers who commissioned them, were pounded out of giant boulders from the Tuxtla Mountains, a volcanic chain some 75 miles west of La Venta as the crow flies, farther by water. Workmen undoubtedly brought the roughly dressed boulders to La Venta by raft. Thus they kept the overland dragging or rolling of the rocks to a minimum—a major factor with sculptures that weigh more than 25 tons apiece.

In 1955 Smithsonian excavations at La Venta uncovered an offering of jade figurines a hand-length high, grouped in a scene suggesting an ancient ritual fossilized forever. This offering was deliberately buried, as was a much larger one of nearly 500 brick-size blocks of imported greenish serpentine. Laid out to form a stylized jaguar mask, they were concealed beneath tons of colored clay. Landscaped mound surfaces at La Venta incorporated clays of striking variety: red, pink, and purple; yellow, orange, brown, tan; olive and blue; and white as well. The sands on plaza floors ranged from white to brown through variants of old rose and cinnamon

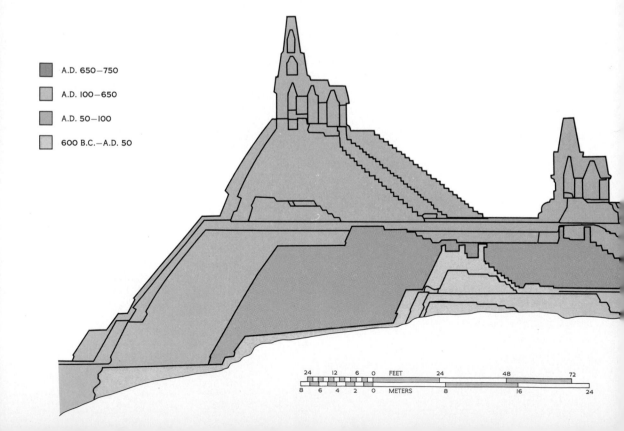

A.D. 650–750

A.D. 100–650

A.D. 50–100

600 B.C.–A.D. 50

24 12 6 0 FEET 24 48 72
8 6 4 2 0 METERS 8 16 24

and red. "A visit to La Venta in its heyday," writes Richard A. Diehl, "must have been a truly psychedelic experience." As another of my colleagues has remarked, "The Olmec may have begun the move to civilization in the New World, but they were really *weird*."

Almost as enigmatic are the builders of Teotihuacán, the grid-planned city founded at about the time of Christ in the basin that now holds the modern colossus of Mexico City. Respectful visitors in Aztec times knew it as "the city of the gods"; tourists today call it "Las Pirámides," and it is still dominated by the twin bulks of the Pyramids of the Sun and the Moon (Aztec names that may reflect the original dedications a thousand years earlier). The latter rises to 150 feet; the former is even higher. Unfortunately, insensitive reconstruction around 1900 destroyed its original profile, but I still find it imposing whenever I visit the site.

(Evidently a natural cave, discovered in 1971, determined the choice of site for the Pyramid of the Sun and the center of the city. No human burial has been discovered to date in either of these two monuments.)

From the top of the Sun Pyramid I can see the "Street of the Dead" (another Aztec name), one of the two major axes of the city; the other runs almost at a right angle to it. In a building just below me, a surveyor's marker has been found: a cross within a circle, like a gunsight but pecked into the plaster floor. Standing here, the town planner could set up an instrument—perhaps as simple as the crossed sticks illustrated in Aztec manuscripts—and take an alignment to the west, where an identical marker has been found in the suburbs. Turning to his right, he could have sighted a pole held above a marker on the hilltop behind the Moon Pyramid.

Having laid out the grid, the planners set about filling it with residential blocks, each about 230 feet square and containing several multi-roomed

PRECEDING PAGES: *In Tikal's Great Plaza, temples taller than the rain forest reflect centuries of construction. As skills developed, styles evolved, and ceremony required, Mesoamericans often set new buildings over existing ones. Archaeology has revealed the stages at Tikal, as shown in section (left) for the North Acropolis. Before A.D. 50, builders raise the first shrines of limestone masonry. In the next half-century a massive platform to hold new structures obliterates the old. About A.D. 200, new work buries everything. In the final stages, temples soar more than 125 feet, with thick rear walls supporting high roof combs. By A.D. 750, at least 10,000 people live in the central city, perhaps as many as 60,000 more nearby. Then, after A.D. 900, comes the dramatic decline of Tikal.*

WILBUR E. GARRETT, N.G.S. STAFF (PRECEDING PAGES)

apartments, lit by small internal courts. An existing community, known now as the "Old City," was incorporated into the northwestern quarter, and the city expanded southward. Its population grew to astonishing numbers for the time—between 125,000 and 200,000 by modern estimate—but the master plan was never fulfilled: The southern quarters are less densely settled than the northern. If there were real-estate speculators around, they may have burned their fingers badly before the city began its steep decline around A.D. 750.

Builders, however, presumably prospered. They had useful materials of volcanic origin at hand, and used them skillfully. The fast-cooled lava called *tezontle*, weatherproof but light in weight, supplied fill as well as structural blocks. *Tepetate*, compacted volcanic ash, figured in foundations, floors, and ceilings. Volcanic gravels probably gave a natural cement for several types of excellent concrete.

Forests were thinned, and destroyed, to supply wood—not only for beams and lintels and pole laths, but also for burning crushed rock to make lime. Plaster of lime or mud coated all the buildings of the city, grand or modest, floors, walls, and roofs; it covered stone facades as well as pole-lath partitions. Did bare rock seem improper or shocking, like an unclad body? Throughout Mesoamerica, architects always gave stone a veneer of stucco or, on sculpture, paint or gleaming polish.

Craftsmanship excepted, we know little about the inhabitants of Teotihuacán. They adorned buildings with murals, but on nonliteral themes. They had no writing—or none that we can understand. Their rulers did not erect monuments to themselves, nor build rich tombs. They remain as thoroughly anonymous as the even more shadowy Olmec.

Yet we know they were in touch with most of Mesoamerica. When René Millon carried out an ambitious survey of Teotihuacán in the 1960s, combining aerial photography with ground survey, he found an area in the western suburbs occupied by people from Oaxaca, a valley some 225 miles to the southeast. In Oaxaca the Zapotec nation had developed a distinctive advanced culture; pottery, and a stone tomb with a stela in Zapotec style, identified the "Oaxaca barrio" for Millon.

Once I flew from Mexico City to Oaxaca; looking down on that crumpled, deforested brown landscape dashed with the green of cornfields and the glint of rivers in the deeper creases, I appreciated the efforts that maintained contact between the two regions when porters and messengers tramped the paths on foot. Within an hour I recognized the Y-shaped junctions of three valleys, the colonial city of Oaxaca de Juarez, and the ruins of its predecessor, the Zapotec capital of Monte Albán, looming on the heights above. I could pick out the terraced platforms that once bore temples and palaces, but these have long since vanished. The

Nourished and sheltered by tradition: Maya children watch a woman prepare tortillas, a timeless staple; the pole-and-thatch type of house antedates 1000 B.C. Stone temples and palaces echoed its shape and angle of roof. FOLLOWING PAGES: Palenque's "Palace"—probably in fact a royal residence and ritual center—expresses Maya genius in full flower. Its forms have unusual elegance. An underground corbel-vault aqueduct led a stream beneath the palace complex.

mounds and foundations that remain prove that local builders had skill and styles of their own, variants of the *talud* (sloping wall) and *tablero* (sunken panel) common in central Mexico.

With a population estimated at 30,000 or less in the fifth through seventh centuries A.D.—and nearly a million cubic yards of fill invested in the civic center—Monte Albán was a force to be reckoned with. About 500 B.C. its site was an unoccupied hilltop; only a century later, the high ground held a small city. Thereafter, this city outranked older centers for a thousand years. Some scholars have suggested that Monte Albán was a sort of Mesoamerican Brasília or Canberra, a "disembedded capital" established at a central, neutral location by agreement of the local polities. I think it reached dominance by the normal means of recorded history, intrigue and war, because its earliest structures hold graphic records of conquest. I have seen lists of humbled rivals represented by their place-name glyphs, and the famous sculptures of slain and mutilated captives known from their grotesque postures as *los danzantes*—the dancers.

Monte Albán has its own evidence of contacts with Teotihuacán: Zapotec glyphs record eight individual Teotihuacanos on carved slabs, and these persons seem to have been concerned with the dedication of a platform in the ceremonial center. What part was Teotihuacán really playing during the Classic Period of A.D. 250-900? Was it a conquering empire like that of the Romans or the Aztecs? A diplomatic dynasty like the Habsburgs of Renaissance Europe, trading daughters for influence until its blood ran in the veins of every ruling house? Or was it primarily a trading state, its prosperity based on control of a major source of obsidian?

The long reach of its merchants was brought home to me in early 1985, as I directed a National Geographic Society-British Museum-Rutgers University excavation at the Maya city of Nohmul, in northern Belize. We were digging a wooden building, a timber-framed hall about 23 feet wide and at least 70 feet long, constructed about A.D. 200-300. The timbers had long since vanished, but we could detect the holes cut for them in the limestone blocks of the high stone platform. We dug them out, and it was easy to imagine the original workman, scraping and gouging away the limestone with a sharp hand-held flint, excavating a full arm's length. As we carefully sifted dirt from one of these post holes, a flash of light glared from a tiny scrap of an obsidian blade. As she examined it to prepare a catalog card, my student Eliza Butler suddenly said, "It's green!" So it was, the olive tint of a beer bottle—and this meant that it had to have come from the source near Teotihuacán, more than 600 miles away, and not from closer outcrops in the Maya highlands, which yield only a black obsidian.

For some years, when scholars thought that Maya civilization began about the time our timber "palace" was being built, they assumed that contact with Teotihuacán inspired the rise of the tropical-forest cities. Now we know more, and better. Evidently the contact ran between two established and complex societies. The Maya were building massive temples, fortifications, and canals between 400 B.C. and A.D. 250. At Cerros, on the northernmost tip of Belize, David Freidel has dated the entire city to before the time of Christ, including a canal nearly 4,000 feet long that de-

fines the ceremonial precinct. Here stand substantial pyramids, smaller than those of Tikal seven centuries later, but still impressive enough.

Yet the Cerros buildings look puny beside the truly colossal structures at El Mirador, a remote site in the rain forest north of Tikal. Discovered by *chicleros* looking for chewing-gum trees in 1926, El Mirador had to wait until 1962 for exploration. Then it was mapped single-handed by Ian Graham, an intrepid Scot who is compiling a catalog of all known Maya hieroglyphic inscriptions.

"When I saw they had used rough boulders instead of evenly cut stone," says Ian, "I thought it must be early—Preclassic—before A.D. 250. The lack of stone-walled buildings on top of the pyramids, and the lack of inscribed monuments, suggested the same thing. But it was so huge, larger than any Classic Maya city I had seen, that I couldn't be sure until I had dug there. In 1970 I was able to prove this hunch, and all the digging since then points the same way." Indeed, El Mirador was at its height during the Late Preclassic Period, when Monte Albán was on the rise and Teotihuacán was still a small town.

By Ian's measurements, El Mirador's major western pyramid is almost 180 feet high, and the massive Danta complex more than a mile away across the central precinct towers more than 200 feet on a base 1,000 feet long. The plaza between them could house more than 50 football games simultaneously, and the temple now called El Tigre (itself covering more than three football fields in area) dates from as early as 150 B.C. Flanking it is a smaller building with jaguar masks taller than a man, and modeled jaguar paws six feet high. Surrounded on three sides by swamps crossed by artificial causeways, still of unknown extent, and with at least four buildings of which any one would cover the entire Great Plaza area of Tikal, El Mirador has a potential hardly tapped so far.

Certainly it offers a striking contrast to the site of Cuello, where I directed a National Geographic Society project in 1978-80. Well known as the earliest Maya settlement so far discovered, Cuello is also fascinating as a small community of the Late Preclassic. Around 400 B.C. its inhabitants decided to convert their ceremonial precinct, a courtyard with buildings on four sides, into something more dramatic: a large raised platform with a pyramid at one end, an open stage for ritual. The rulers had the courtyard filled in with rubble; and in this, below the floor of the new platform, they laid a sacrifice of more than 20 young men. Offerings placed with the hacked-up skeletons included six carved tubes of bone, possibly the handles of ceremonial fans. Four of the tubes bore the design of a woven mat; and the mat (*pop* to the ancient Maya) was the symbol of rulership. Thus we find, possibly as the earliest example, the iconography of royal power in the Maya lowlands.

This is especially significant because in Mesoamerica the rulers *were* the builders. Without their ambitious projects, men would probably have

FOLLOWING PAGES: Children romp where ritual prevailed at Copán. Sloping-sided ball court and surrounding temples attest to ancient ceremonies held in the sacred center. Men using a rubber ball performed, but not in sport. Their play held cosmic significance and may have represented movements of celestial bodies.

Visitors at Uxmal respect the steep rise of steps leading up the pyramid of the so-called House of the Magician. A corbel-vault passage runs underneath, with a remnant of an earlier vault still in place. Corbeling limited the height and span of a vault, creating long, narrow rooms; in "palaces" the technique required thick partition walls to help support the roof. Often, multiple doorways admitted light to windowless interiors. Normally, Maya masons used a lime mortar. At Uxmal, mortar and rubble formed a fill comparable to good concrete. Finely cut stone faced these structures—but Maya builders covered their work with plaster and painted that a strong red or the famous, bright "Maya blue." Royal regalia took color from brilliant feathers; a macaw at Copán suggests the possibilities.

contented themselves with modest homes for their families—and their deities: houses like those we still use in camp. Peter Harrison of the University of New Mexico, who began his career excavating the palace of Ah Cacau at Tikal, has shown how all Maya buildings spring from the basic dwelling with its supporting platform that assures a dry floor, its lashed-pole walls, and its thatch roof. Repeated side to side, it forms the range buildings or "palaces" of Uxmal and Palenque. The more I see of Maya buildings, the more I admire the ingenuity with which these three elements are enlarged or shrunk, ornamented, translated from perishable materials into enduring stone. When I compare their artistic achievements with those of the Classical Greeks I studied in college, I remind myself that the Maya had to work with tools of wood or stone—their only metal took the form of jewelry—without draft animals to haul a load of stone, without wheels or pulleys to raise it. And they worked well.

Limestone underlies the Maya lowlands. Men learned the art of cutting and dressing it, of stacking the blocks and edging them together to form a corbel "vault." They crushed and burned it to make plaster. (On the small scale of Cuello, I can sense the work of individual craftsmen laying plaster in the courtyard: a skilled mason followed by a sloppy son and a more conscientious grandson.) In the hill region called the Puuc, at such cities as Uxmal, they developed excellent mortar into true concrete—if the veneer stones fell off, the walls would stand true and solid. "At Cobá," says my colleague George Stuart, "their stucco was better than the stone. If you hit it with a metal hammer, it rings like a piece of iron.

"Even the old sloppy Postclassic stuff works," he adds. "Even Tulum—it looks like a caricature of a Classic site, but it has stood up surprisingly well to time and storms and salt air."

Today many of the Maya cities rest shrouded in jungle, with vines and tree roots forcing the stones apart. In the ninth century their civilization collapsed, for causes still uncertain. I suspect that overpopulation, strain on food resources, malnutrition and disease among the lower classes, and

Maya villagers of Bolonchen (Nine Wells) get water 210 feet underground in the dry season when surface sources fail in limestone country. In 1842 artist-explorer Frederick Catherwood drew this scene; his companion John Lloyd Stephens called the ladder 70-odd feet of "rough trunks of saplings lashed together." Similar ladders and scaffolds probably served ancient builders; a graffito at Tikal implies their use. In a book that gave Maya ruins their modern fame, Stephens called corbeling the "most simple mode of covering over a void space." A rare example in fired brick (left) appears as a vault at Comalcalco, in a coastal area that lacked usable stone. Art and architectural style suggest that this city was an outpost of Palenque, about a hundred miles to the southeast. Brick masonry "does not appear at any other documented Maya site," writes architect George F. Andrews, but "it is not a large step to move from fired-clay pottery to fired-clay bricks. . . ."

political stresses all combined in a great descending spiral of social decay. Some centers in Yucatán flourished longer. Chichén Itzá achieved between A.D. 800 and 1100 a dynamic blend of local culture and elements from the central highlands of Mexico.

There, two centuries later, the rising power was the Aztec Empire, which spread down to the Pacific coast to grab a cacao-growing region and thus control the precious beans used not only for chocolate but also as a currency. The Maya were next on the Aztec hit list in 1519, when the Spanish saved them for a fate worse than death.

Hernán Cortés and his tiny band of conquistadors were stunned by the sight of the Aztec capital of Tenochtitlán. It lay in a great lake on man-made islands, linked to the shore by causeways. One of these carried two masonry aqueducts to supply, as Cortés noted, "a stream of very good fresh water, as wide as a man's body." A nine-mile dike of stone slabs protected the city from floods. This, said Aztec chroniclers, was the work of Nezahualcoyotl, king of Texcoco on the eastern shore, the Renaissance man of Aztec Mexico—poet, philosopher, and probably the only pre-Columbian architect or engineer we can know as more than a name. He designed the work after a dreadful inundation in A.D. 1449; and, with his ally the lord of Tenochtitlán, began the work in person.

Victorious after a long struggle, the Spanish razed the city, tearing down temples and palaces and filling in canals. Yet because the heavy buildings had always been subsiding into the soft muddy soil, some were already safely buried when Cortés came. Under the colonial streets the structures of Tenochtitlán occasionally assert themselves. There is a striking instance near the Zócalo, the principal square where recent excavations have exposed the great temple of Tlaloc and Huitzilopochtli with its successive periods of building superimposed and nested like Chinese boxes. From the temple precinct ran the avenue and causeway on which the Spaniards had escaped in the famous night of sorrow, *El Noche Triste*. Later a Spanish church was built, partly on and partly off the roadway. Earthquakes have opened conspicuous cracks between the rear of the church, on yielding subsoil, and the front, secure on Aztec foundations.

From the first, the peoples of the highlands faced challenges unlike those found in the lowlands: volcanoes and earthquakes instead of rampant jungle. They met them in varying—and effective—ways. Yet their buildings, from Olmec to Aztec, retain something of a common Mesoamerican tradition. By virtue of shared ancestry or shared religious ideas, the builders of ancient Mexico and the Maya lands lived in an intellectual space as broad as that through which their merchants traded the green obsidian of Teotihuacán.

Enacting an ancient ritual, men called voladores *whirl downward at El Tajín, a Huastec city. Possibly before A.D. 300, its builders piled up a boulder-and-clay core; later architects added stone slabs to create a pyramid with 365 window-like niches; these make dramatic play with light and shade—and lessen overall weight.*
FOLLOWING PAGES: Mexico City surrounds the Templo Major, principal shrine in the Aztec capital of Tenochtitlán. Nested stairs reveal repeated rebuilding on unstable ground; ritual use ended abruptly with Spanish conquest in 1521.

DAVID HISER (OPPOSITE); MARK GODFREY/
ARCHIVE PICTURES (FOLLOWING PAGES)

SOUTH AMERICA

SOUTH AMERICA

By Ron Fisher
Photographs by William Albert Allard

T**he condor is a lofty bird, a wide-winged seeker of high places in the high Andes of South America. It can fly 35 miles an hour, and climb to 15,000 feet. It seldom flaps its massive wings, which may stretch ten feet, but soars instead on mountain thermals, and the sound of the wind in those wings can be heard a hundred yards away. It's an ugly bird with a nightmare face, barely changed from Pleistocene times a million years ago; and it is becoming rare these days. But archaeologists in the Andes often find the images of condors woven into ancient fabrics or cut into the rocks of Indian ruins. The Indians made flutes from the wing bones of the condor. Christians new to the New World went out of their way to kill the big birds—symbols, they thought, of the Indians' pagan gods.

A condor aloft in the Andes in the 1400s would have witnessed, in the mountain heights and river valleys below, the flowering of a remarkable civilization. It began when a tribe of Indians living around what is now Cuzco in Peru began conquering other tribes, absorbing them as subjects. We know the victors by the title of their rulers, the Incas. At its height, the Inca Empire stretched nearly 3,000 miles along the western edge of South America, reaching from what is now southern Colombia through all of Peru and southward into Chile.

The Incas are remembered for a number of reasons: for the strength and character of their emperors; for the gold and silver they wrested from the cold Andes; for the panpipes and drums of their eerie, breathy music; for the few words they contributed to our language, like quinine and alpaca; for the image of a farmer, in woven cap and poncho, herding llamas along a wind-blown ridge.

But it was in their buildings, and especially their stonework, that the Incas achieved degrees of skill and beauty seldom surpassed. Prying huge stones from hillsides, shaping them, transporting them over carefully constructed roads and ramps across miles of rough terrain, fitting them together in seamless perfection, the Inca builders created in the few short decades of their empire structures that retain their power to amaze. Today, when people see Inca stonework for the first time, they marvel: "Isn't it beautiful?" And then they ask, "How on earth did they do it?"

To find out, I sought help, oddly enough, in the classrooms and high-tech computer laboratories of California.

On the pleasant Berkeley campus of the University of California, I

PRECEDING PAGES: Adobe walls of Chan Chan, an ancient city in the northern desert of Peru, frame their caretaker, Santos Villa. Though rebuilt, these walls probably reflect Chan Chan's appearance at its florescence about 1400, when it was the capital of South America's pre-Columbian Chimu Empire.

Arid coastal plain and towering Andes seem unlikely settings for South America's first great civilizations. Yet for 1,500 years, successive empires produced awe-inspiring monuments, and feats of engineering that conquered the terrain. Earlier achievements culminated in the brief, brilliant Inca Empire that stretched 3,000 miles, from modern Colombia to central Chile, until destroyed by Spanish conquistadors.

found Professor Jean-Pierre Protzen, head of the department of architecture. In smooth Gallic accents, he said, "I wondered, too, 'How did they do it?' and decided that the best way to find out was to try it myself." He went to Peru, visited ancient quarries, and tried his hand at stone-carving, Inca style, with Inca tools. "I easily found quite a lot of tools they used, simple river cobbles that were used as hammerstones.

"The hammers are mostly quartzite, granite, or olivine basalt. They are almost exactly the same hardness—5.5 on Mohs' scale—as the andesite they were used on, but they are tougher. Andesite shatters under the blow; for a rough cut, I could just drop the hammer. Once you get the hang of it, it goes remarkably fast. I cut three sides and five edges of a small block in just 90 minutes. I'm sure with experience you could go much faster. Fitting two stones together was more tedious—a matter of trial and error. It took me another 90 minutes to achieve a tight fit.

"When you get to Peru, take a look at the stonework in Cuzco. It's the most remarkable the world has ever seen, and the sort of work I was attempting to duplicate."

At the other end of the technological scale from stone hammers and chisels, in the heady world of computers, another Californian is studying pre-Inca engineering. I found Charles Ortloff in the low-slung building of an engineering firm in Silicon Valley, near San José. His specialties are structural analysis and the mechanics of fluids.

"In the north of Peru," he told me, "every major valley has hundreds of kilometers of irrigation canals dating from early centuries A.D. up to Inca times in the middle of the 15th century. Great floods periodically damaged these systems. And remember, the coast there is very active, seismically and tectonically, so as the ground rose or subsided over the centuries, irrigation canals had to be rebuilt to accommodate the change. If your irrigation system is collapsing, you have to invent a higher technology—just as we do—to make it work better. Excuse me a second."

He turned to a computer that was drawing colored diagrams on its screen. "We're designing a new vehicle for the Marine Corps and this is part of it." The computer hummed and glowed as he dealt with it.

"Anyway, that led the Indians to more sophisticated hydraulic controls. I put the shape of one segment of one canal into a computer and asked it to compute the flow of water. I also built a scale model of that segment and ran water through it. Instruments measured the water's velocity and height, and sawdust on the surface showed currents and eddies. The computer and the scale model agreed: The channel had been purposefully designed to control the velocity of the water by the roughness or smoothness of the walls, local slope, and variations of cross-section geometry. No matter how fast water went in, it always came out more slowly at the other end. Accomplishing that represented many hundreds of years of experience in fluid mechanics, and also involved understanding a variety of very sophisticated hydraulic principles. Evidently there was a corps of people in charge of the irrigation system—surveyors, hydraulic engineers—who did what we would call systems analysis. And did it very well.

"When you're in Peru, try to get up into the north to see some of these old canals. They were really amazing."

But who were these people, these movers and builders?

My first guide was Dr. Christopher Donnan, director of the UCLA Museum of Cultural History. I found him in a cool basement office, its walls hung with assorted artifacts. He was looking forward to his third season of digging at a site called Pacatnamú on the north coast of Peru. It had two periods of flowering, he explained, roughly between A.D. 600 and 1000 and between 1100 and 1400. "Meet me there later in the summer, and I'll show you around."

It was winter in Peru a few weeks later,   *(Continued on page 105)*

A Peruvian brickmaker can produce half a ton a day. His ancestors used these same materials—silt, sand, and water—to make bricks for their cities, walls, and temples; local builders will use these in modern homes near Trujillo.
FOLLOWING PAGES: Eroded stumps of giant huacas, *or sacred structures, rise in the Moche Valley.* Huaca del Sol *(foreground) ranked as the largest solid-brick platform of its kind: Some 143 million adobe bricks went into it. Beyond lies Huaca de la Luna, a sister shrine. Moche villagers built them two thousand years ago.*

Recently rebuilt, a ceremonial plaza lies within the eroded walls of one of the ten compounds at the core of Chan Chan, one of South America's first true cities, and the largest. It once covered about 7.8 square miles. Each compound apparently housed a ruler and his entourage and had a garden, huge wells, and many storerooms; at the ruler's death, the compound became his mausoleum. Stylized creatures (right)—possibly sea otters—frolic on an ancient adobe wall.

when we strolled across the desolate site, with desert breezes kicking up sand and dust. Pacatnamú is right on the coast, on a triangular plateau 120 feet above a narrow beach and a river valley. It took me a minute to realize that the humps we were walking over were man-made walls and pyramids covered by the relentless drift of the coastal desert. There were little seashells lying about, and ancient corncobs the size of paperclips, and minute scraps of fabrics hundreds of years old. And here, as at nearly every archaeological site in Peru, pot hunters called *huaqueros* have plundered many graves, scattering fragments as they search for treasure.

I walked with Chris to the top of a mound—a *huaca*, holy place or thing. It is one of about 50, some much larger than others, most of them within rectangular enclosures. "My theory is this," he explained. "The site was abandoned by the Moche people, the first occupants, around A.D. 1000, possibly because of heavy rains that would have played havoc with the adobe construction. Then, about a hundred years later, a threat of some kind arose. The people from local villages saw the defensive potential of Pacatnamú, moved in, and built walls and ditches for defense. I think that perhaps each village, to satisfy its religious needs, built its own huaca. The richest and largest villages would have built the largest huacas because they could summon the most workmen.

"You do wonder what sort of lives they could have led, with so much of their GNP devoted to defense and religion.

"Eventually, I think, the threat—whatever it was—went away, and the site was abandoned again."

Next morning, the first morning of the dig, Chris set half a dozen of the Peruvian workmen to digging post holes for a guardhouse, a makeshift shelter for wheelbarrows and shovels. One of them turned up the fragments of a shattered pot—Moche.

"Move the house to the left," Chris told them. Again they began digging, but again stopped almost immediately. More pottery, with old fabric and disintegrating reeds—the material of Moche caskets. "Never mind the shack," said Chris. "Let's see what we've got here."

He quickly laid out a grid of string and stakes and put the crew to serious digging. As the hot sun climbed into the sky, the desert was still but for the scraping of shovels. Grave after grave appeared. *"Tomba!"* a man would cry, and we would gather round.

"Of all the things we could find, an unlooted Moche cemetery would be the best," said Chris. "There's never been one found in this valley." In three hours we located six unlooted graves.

Chris gave me a trowel and a brush, and put me to work with the team uncovering a grave. A potbellied vessel emerged, with the face of a bird on it. Then more and more of a reed casket appeared. There was a small gap between two of the thick reeds, and I could see something hard and yellowish. "What am I seeing here?" I asked John Verano, the young

Icon of white granite, 15 feet high, portrays an eerie deity—half man, half jaguar. Called El Lanzón, *it stands embedded in dark local rock, among walls built around it, at the heart of a temple complex at Chavín de Huántar, in Peru. Artisans of the Chavín culture built this around 850 B.C., high in the Andes.*

physical anthropologist, who was working nearby. "That's his skull," John said. And suddenly I found myself standing up and taking a step backward. *His skull.*

He gave substance to the remainder of my time in Peru. Whoever he was, and however he came to be there, undisturbed for a thousand years until I came along, I kept him in mind as I traveled about his country. I got acquainted with some of his ancestors, and some of his descendants.

The ancient building techniques of South America may have culminated in the Inca civilization, but there were builders on the continent doing remarkable work long before them. Almost three thousand years ago, the first great South American civilization—the Chavín Cult—spread across much of Peru. It left at least one great structure, a pyramid temple at Chavín de Huántar deep in the Andes.

I hired a car on the coast to take me to Huaraz, and for six hours the old Pontiac inched upward, wheezing and coughing. Every 20 minutes we stopped to refill the boiling radiator from a roadside stream. I found a guide—"I'm the only perfect bilingual in Huaraz," he told me—and the next day we crossed the continental divide, to Chavín de Huántar.

H ere, between an unstable mountainside and the turbulent Mosna River, are grass-grown sunken plazas, framed by steep-walled platforms. The largest structure, a pyramidal temple, is a massive building of mortarless stone masonry, about 250 feet square and 45 feet high. Its three stories are riddled with narrow passageways, right angles, cul-de-sacs; it even has air vents. I ducked my head and followed my guide and his hissing lantern through the dark, cool maze of interior galleries, stairs, ramps, and ventilation shafts. In one small chamber is an astounding work of art, a monolith 15 feet high. Now called *El Lanzón,* it stands like a lancehead or dagger driven into the stone floor. Stylized carvings—fierce, elegant, and assured—portray a snarling god with the fangs of a great cat, with claws on hands and feet, with writhing serpents for hair.

A complex but coherent structure, the temple must have been planned as an entity. Its outer walls consist of well-cut rectangular stones, skillfully polished, laid in even courses. Each row of large blocks is set between two layers of much thinner stones: a telling, rhythmic contrast.

Far to the south, near the shore of Lake Titicaca, lies another ruin that predates the Incas—Tiahuanaco, near La Paz in Bolivia. A sturdy little train took me there through miles of gray drizzle. I watched llamas and alpacas resting on soggy hillsides, chewing their cuds. Little boys—mock desperados—attacked the train at desolate stations, where sleet pattered against the windows.

At the upper limits of human habitation, at 13,000 feet, where the air is thin and the treeless plain unsuited to crops, Tiahuanaco developed between A.D. 200 to 600. Little is known about the lives of the people who built it, but something of their skill. They constructed its walls of basalt and sandstone quarried nearby. The great blocks, some weighing a hundred tons, were smoothly fitted together. An enormous gateway—now called the Gateway of the Sun—is the site's most famous relic. Carved from a single block of andesite, it is 10 feet high, 12 feet 6 inches wide, and

weighs about 10 tons. It is decorated with stylized motifs—condors, warriors, sun-men—carved in low relief. In the nearby modern town, many doorways and walls are built of stones taken from the ancient city; against some, dark-eyed Indians rest, solemn as a sculptor's images.

Perhaps the most impressive early city in Peru is Chan Chan, capital of the Chimu Empire that arose just down the coast from Pacatnamú. It thrived for a good four centuries, succumbing to the Incas around 1470. The city, with some 30,000 people in its prime, was the largest known in ancient Peru, covering nearly eight square miles. It eventually held ten large, walled compounds; each in turn, apparently, served as a palace for a living ruler and a center of cult for him in death.

Chan Chan is made of millions of sun-dried bricks, manufactured from the land the city rests on, so that it has the texture and the dun hue of its setting. On the compound walls, adobe friezes feature stylized sea creatures, reminders of the surf thumping nearby.

It was difficult to imagine crops ripening in the hot wind-blown desert around Chan Chan, but crops there were, thanks to the remarkable irrigation system Charles Ortloff had told me about. I visited one canal he had mentioned at Ascope, not far from Trujillo. Pedro Puerta, local artist and historian, helped me find it. I saw its celebrated mile-long aqueduct, essentially a huge snake of earth 40 feet high, with a shallow channel along its back. All told, the Ascope canal meanders from interior mountains to valley farmland, a distance of some 40 miles. It averages, roughly, less than one degree of slope per mile, an incredible achievement.

The channel ditch was dry, its walls crumbling and bushes growing in it, when I walked beside it with Pedro and two young farmers, Juan and Humberto, whose fields bordered the aqueduct. Humberto asked, through Pedro, how many kilograms of corn we get per hectare in the States, and I was sorry I couldn't tell him. He gets about 6,000. (We average 6,506, as I learned later.)

"Burrowing owls, making their nests in the sides of the canal, dig holes that let the water out," Pedro commented, and we saw one of the big brown birds emerge from its burrow and fly off across a cornfield. (Did Chan Chan's specialists include anti-owl patrols?)

With Pedro I sampled *chicha,* the ancient corn beer that the Incas brewed. It smelled like apple cider and had a slightly sour taste, as if freshly made—which no doubt it was.

If the Incas were the Romans of pre-Columbian America, Cuzco was their Rome. According to imperial legend, the city was founded by Manco Capac, the Son of the Sun and the first Inca. The Sun, pitying the earth, sent his heir to spread culture and enlightenment, with a daughter to be his wife. This pair emerged from the waters of Lake Titicaca and began a long search for a place to found their kingdom. At last they chose a fertile valley, the "navel of the earth," and called it Cuzco. (Archaeologists, however, who date Inca beginnings to late in the 12th century A.D., have found evidence of people living in the area at least a thousand years earlier.)

The Incas never developed a written language, the wheel, or the arch, but they had a genius for organization and administration. From their capital, roads ran to all corners of their empire, and along them hurried runners with news and messages.

An enormous work force—in a population of perhaps six million—was

available for *mita,* or labor service. Because the Incas had no money, taxes were paid in the form of service in the army, in the retinue of the emperor and the nobility, or as a laborer on public works. Every able-bodied man from age 25 to 50 had to do his bit, and this element was divided into units based on ten—ten men in a "platoon," ten platoons in a "company," and so forth. Administrators could quickly and easily assemble a force to fight a battle, or build a bridge, or repair an irrigation system.

Such units constructed the agricultural terraces, "glories of Inca engineering" as one scholar calls them, that minimized dangers of landslips and concentrated fertile soil in easily worked plots. Retaining walls of *pirca,* roughly dressed fieldstone set in clay mortar, still mark the slopes.

Despite local frosts, floods, and droughts, the empire produced huge surpluses of food as well as textiles, weapons, pottery, and all the necessities of life—to say nothing of luxuries. These goods were kept in storehouses, structures with pirca walls and thatch roofs, along the network of roads. (A single remote site in what is now Bolivia had 2,400 storehouses: all round, all 10 feet in diameter, sited 17 feet apart in rows 31 feet apart so that fire could not spread from thatch to thatch.) Provincial towns had spacious stone halls called *kallankas,* places of assembly for festivals in rainy weather and barracks for troops or labor units on the march.

The finest stonemasons came in shifts to Cuzco, where examples of their artistry can still be seen. They worked in two distinctive styles. In the polygonal style, irregular stones—limestone, granite or diorite, or whatever—were fitted together, no two of identical size or shape. In the coursed style, the stones—almost always andesite—were cut into uniform rectangles and laid in regular courses, like bricks. In both, however, the masons cut a slight bevel along the edges: Thus a thin line of shadow defines each stone, and even the plainest wall escapes monotony.

Apparently the Incas preferred the symmetry of the coursed style; today many people find the polygonal walls more impressive. A 17th-

Warp and weft of fibers—reeds for a boat, wool for a blanket or poncho— keep alive ancient Andean arts. This boat-builder on Lake Titicaca lashes bundles of totora reeds, common on the lake's shores, that will float for perhaps a year before becoming waterlogged. In Huatajata, Bolivia, a woman creates a colorful fabric. Her bowler's style may survive from Britons who came to build railroads.
FOLLOWING PAGES: *Indians blend Christian and pagan rituals at the feast of Corpus Christi in Cuzco, former capital of the Incas. The cathedral's baroque doorway incorporates features from classical antiquity—a rounded Roman arch, the Corinthian columns of Greece.*

century Spanish scholar wrote: "although they appear rougher they seem to me to have been far more difficult to build.... One can imagine the amount of work involved in making them interlock.... it must have been necessary to remove and replace them repeatedly to test them. And with stones as large as these, it becomes clear how many people and how much suffering must have been involved."

More recently, experimenting with his small andesite blocks, Professor Protzen tried his hand at joining irregular shapes. He found that dust from the pounding gave a useful check on the fit; it lay loose where the surfaces did not quite meet, and was compressed where they did. Moreover, practice sharpened his eye for a good match of surfaces. Trial and error was the basic technique, he concluded; it might be slow, but the Incas, as he has pointed out, did not have our notions of time.

In planning their capital, they laid out the city in the shape of a reclining puma. Near its heart is the main square, the Plaza de Armas. It was much larger in Inca days, but even now is the focus of life in Cuzco. The people have the solemn good looks, high cheekbones, and dark hair of their Inca ancestors. Women sell handicrafts, and ragged shoeshine boys work the crowds. Girls with babies slung in ponchos on their backs, and bemused llamas on tethers, pose for tourist photos, and wily pickpockets

exact a stealthy tribute from the unwary. More typically, people welcome visitors with shy charm. While I was in town a number of hotels were sponsoring a soccer tournament. I watched as my hotel won the game, won the tournament, even won a huge trophy. The players spotted me and, politely, included me in the celebration. We trooped into our hotel manager's office for drinks and speeches, then into the staff dining room for more speeches and warm beer, then into the nightspots of Cuzco for serious celebrating. Late in the night, in a smoky little tavern, the mood turned melancholy. A guitar appeared and one of the waiters, Juan, played while another sang. One of their songs was *"El Cóndor Pasa"*—a song familiar in the States, written in Cuzco. "The Andes witnessed your birth, condor," he sang, "and mine, too. You will always be a wandering soul, condor, as will I." I leaned back and realized, with a start, that my shoulders were touching the cool stones of an Inca wall.

Whatever style was used, the Inca masonry was wonderfully strong. When earthquakes periodically rattle Peru, it is the modern structures that come tumbling down; the Inca walls remain.

Olga Villagarcia, who teaches linguistics at the university in Cuzco, showed me some of the ancient sites outside of town, starting with Sacsahuaman. If Cuzco is shaped like a puma, Sacsahuaman is its head. Once

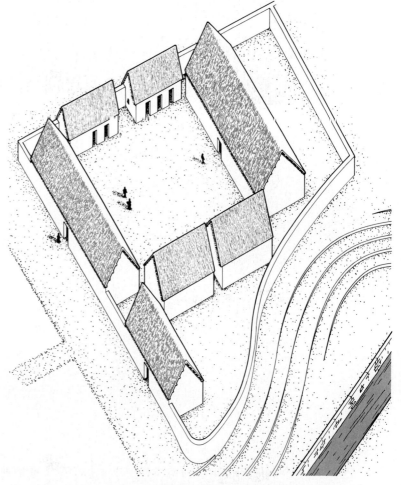

Ageless stone, carved and laid by Incas for their most sacred temple, today supports a Catholic church. At the height of the Inca Empire, the structures of the Coricancha (drawing) bore finely thatched roofs of grasses, reeds, and rattan with elegantly braided interiors. The stone walls wore sheaths of solid gold. Spanish conquerors in the 1530s stripped the temple of its treasures, including idols, votive statues, and at least 700 sheets of gold, each weighing four and a half pounds. Melted into ingots—along with tons of silver—it filled Spanish coffers in the Old World. In 1534, the site of the Coricancha was turned over to the Dominicans, directors of the Spanish Inquisition; it has held a Christian sanctuary ever since. Much Inca stonework remains, mostly inside the church, together with this curved section of wall in the so-called coursed style— often considered the finest surviving example of Inca masonry.

FROM GRAZIANO GASPARINI AND LUISE MARGOLIES

this was both shrine and stronghold, a hill fortified with three immense terraces. These, built in easily defended zigzags, may have represented the puma's teeth. The Incas' most imposing stonework is found here. Hiram Bingham, who discovered Machu Picchu, wrote that Sacsahuaman was "perhaps the most extraordinary structure built by ancient man in the Western Hemisphere. In fact, as an achievement of engineering, it stands without parallel in American antiquity. . . . The determination and the perseverance of the builders stagger the imagination." Smaller blocks in the polygonal walls, he wrote, weigh ten or twenty tons, larger blocks two hundred tons, and the largest three hundred.

In 1580 a Jesuit described these rocks as "more like lumps of mountain than building stone," and some Spaniards concluded that they must have been moved and set in place by sorcerers. Those early visitors saw much more than remains today: towers above and tunnels below, with a labyrinth of chambers to keep the imperial treasures safe. But after the empire fell, the site became a quarry for later builders. "Before the great earthquake in May 1950," Olga told me, "you could easily buy a truckload of stones from Sacsahuaman if you wanted to."

We visited the town of Chinchero, once a country resort for one of the reigning Incas. The main square is renowned for its huge wall, which holds 12 of the trapezoidal niches characteristic of Inca architecture. In

niche or window or doorway, this shape—wider at the base than at the top—identifies an ancient structure as Inca, for architectural style was virtually uniform throughout the empire. As the Venezuelan scholars Graziano Gasparini and Luise Margolies have said, there was in effect a single designer, and "it was the state."

On our drive back to Cuzco, we picked up a schoolboy trudging up a hill. He looked like the littlest Inca, with his straight black hair and noble nose, and he was struck dumb to find himself with a gringo. But when we stopped near his home, he gathered his courage and made quite a little speech—mostly, according to Olga—dealing with Peruvian-American friendship. He spoke in Quechua, the language of the Incas.

The language has endured, as no doubt the Incas thought their empire would, but in fact their civilization is remarkable for its brevity. It endured barely a hundred years, from about 1438, when Pachacuti, the first emperor, began his reign, to 1532, when two sounds foreign to Peru were heard—the clip-clop of horses' hooves, and voices speaking in Spanish.

On May 16 of that year of Our Lord, Francisco Pizarro and about two hundred conquistadors marched into Peru, searching for gold. Fortuitously, they found the empire in disarray. An emperor had died, and a power struggle was under way between two of his sons. The Spaniards lured the victor—Atahuallpa—into a trap and killed enough Indians to show they meant business. They demanded a ransom for Atahuallpa, and he offered to fill a room of his palace once with gold and twice with silver in return for his freedom. By mid-1533, it is estimated, more than 24 tons of treasure had been collected: idols, jewelry, drinking vessels, dismantled altars and fountains. Nevertheless, in one of a long series of betrayals, Pizarro had Atahuallpa taken into the public square and put to death.

Over the next few years, the Spaniards consolidated their power. Again and again they defeated the Indians in warfare—though the Incas were supreme warriors against other tribes, they could not prevail against Spanish armor and horses. Shrewdly, the Spaniards set up puppet emperors, who gave the new regime a semblance of legitimacy.

Some of its subjects fled eastward, into the forests of the Amazon headwaters, but many accepted the rule of the invaders. The country continued to function, after a fashion: Imperial storehouses no longer held supplies in reserve for the people, but crops got planted, bridges got repaired, fabrics got woven. The objects of precious metals the Spaniards melted into ingots and shipped to Spain; the Indians they enslaved; the country they divided into fiefdoms where their authority was absolute. It was not until 1824 that Peru again became an independent country.

But despite 300 years of their presence, there is at least one Inca city the Spaniards never found. To get there now from Cuzco you take a little train that puffs and clatters and rocks like a dinghy alongside the green and foamy Urubamba River, a tributary (Continued on page 124)

"Technically and aesthetically astounding," one historian called Inca masonry. A famous example, the "Stone of Twelve Angles" in Cuzco, has a dozen corners carved with absolute precision. Earthquakes periodically shake the city, but walls of Inca stonework stand as solidly as on the day of their completion.

Like jagged teeth, the terraced walls of Sacsahuaman guard an Inca stronghold. Some 20,000 men labored for decades to construct this citadel, which overlooks Cuzco. Some of the individual stones stand 19 feet tall and weigh more than a hundred tons. Masons used stone tools to cut the blocks, wood or bronze prybars and sheer manpower to move them, trial and error to fit them together. Commentators have noted that sometimes Inca masons seemed deliberately to choose the most difficult solution to a problem— almost as if showing off. Over the centuries, Sacsahuaman has been nearly dismantled by Cuzco builders, who robbed the site of all but the largest stones. "It was a monument that deserved to be spared such devastation," wrote a chronicler who played in the ruins as a boy. Engineering on a smaller scale, a fountain still splashes at nearby Ollantaytambo. The stepped design came from Tiahuanaco with skilled stonemasons pressed into work gangs to serve an Inca emperor.

Stonework terraces of Ollantaytambo climb toward a once-fortified Inca temple above the Urubamba Valley. Spaniards attacked this stronghold in 1536: "We found it so well fortified that it was a horrifying sight," wrote one. The Indians fired small stones from slingshots, hurled down larger ones, and diverted river water to flood the valley. A wounded horse tumbled down the stairs at left, knocking down horsemen who followed. The rebel emperor Manco Inca appeared

on the terraces "on horseback keeping control of his army." The Indians successfully repulsed the Spaniards this time, but a year later, outnumbered, they abandoned Ollantaytambo—"with many tears, sobbing, and sighs"—and retreated into the jungle, relinquishing their empire to the hated invaders. For years Manco Inca's sons ruled a defiant outpost state, which they called Vilcabamba.

of the Amazon. After more than three hours you disembark and board a bus for a 20-minute ride that switchbacks up a mountain. You get off at a small hotel, pay your fee, walk up a hill, through a gate, around a corner, and there you are—Machu Picchu, the fabled city of the children of the sun, the lost city of the Incas, one of the true wonders of the world.

It is a small city—a village, really—on a saddle between two mountain peaks. Ancient agricultural terraces stairstep neatly up one side of the ridge, and ruins spill down its flanks. It seems both an impossible place to build a city, and a perfect place. I began to understand why there have been such wild theories to explain Inca engineering, for here the effort of building seems genuinely superhuman.

I timed my visit carefully, to be as nearly alone as possible, and strolled peaceably through the ruins, watched over by a dusty alpaca named Bantu, tamed by years of contact with the tourists. I could look straight down 2,000 feet to the river or look straight up 2,000 feet to lush green peaks. Clouds wafted up from the river and swirled among mountaintops. Swallows darted through the ruins, and a flock of green parrots, as raucous as children, winged by over the gorge.

Machu Picchu's mysteries extend to its function. It may have been a military outpost, an imperial retreat, a ceremonial center, a refuge for holy women of Inca cult. Whatever it was, it was important, for the stonework here is among the Incas' finest.

I sat out a rainstorm under the thatch of a little stone structure called the watchman's hut. Thunder pealed in the mountains around me, and mist glided over the ancient stones. Then shafts of sunlight bathed the highest point of the city, the *inti huatana*. This is a masterwork of abstract sculpture, undoubtedly sacred to the Incas' father the Sun.

The jungle was already reclaiming Machu Picchu when the Spaniards committed a final heartbreaking crime—or act of state. For nearly 40 years, heirs of the free Incas had maintained the cause of resistance at a jungle hideout called Vilcabamba. Finally, in 1572, the Spanish sent a powerful force to take the little city. They captured young Inca Tupac Amaru and his pregnant wife, and carried him in chains back to Cuzco. Within three days, while Quechua-speaking monks and priests instructed him in the Christian faith, the viceroy had him tried for murder in trumped-up proceedings. He was baptized, convicted, and—to the horror of Spanish churchmen and laity alike—beheaded in the public square. Thousands of Indians gathered to wail for him. As his warm blood seeped onto the cold stones of Cuzco, the Inca dynasty ended.

Today, swallows and parrots may swirl in the skies above Machu Picchu, but the condors are gone.

High above the Apurimac River, a Peruvian farmer repairs a bridge made of some 22,000 feet of hand-spun rope. The Incas built such now-rare spans throughout Peru. PAGES 120-121: Timeless stone houses, their thatch roofs long gone, catch the afternoon sun at Machu Picchu, fabled mountain city of the Incas. PAGES 122-123: A supreme achievement of its ancient builders, Machu Picchu clings to a verdant, mountain-rimmed saddle high above the Urubamba River. It escaped destruction because the Spanish never found it.

INDIA
AND
SOUTHEAST
ASIA

INDIA AND SOUTHEAST ASIA

By Joyce Stewart
Photographs by Richard A. Cooke III

Clad in the colors of sunrise, dancing and blowing conch shells, devotees led the way on a path garlanded with marigolds to a new Hindu temple in Jaipur, India. I followed barefoot in the throng, across moist young grass, over rough jute mats, up steps of sun-warmed marble strewn with rose and frangipani petals. Crushed underfoot, they exuded a fragrance so sweet I could taste it. Inside, pungent smoke assailed my nostrils, and the walls rang with the joyous shouts of worshipers as priests chanted prayers and performed a fire ritual of a type that may be almost 4,000 years old. Thus they sanctified two smiling marble images, richly attired in vermilion and gold, that the divine might take up abode in this holy of holies.

This ceremony, held on an auspicious spring day in 1985, invoked Narayana (an aspect of Vishnu) and his consort, Lakshmi, inviting them to dwell in a temple built by a family of industrialists who carry on the tradition of wealthy donors. And the tradition of hereditary craftsmen also lives on. I was told that Muslim stonecutters, who claim descent from artisans who worked on the Taj Mahal, carved the gleaming white marble in the temple, whose 125-foot spire soars above the sanctuary like the mythical Mount Meru so sacred to the Hindus.

In the dazzling human diversity of the subcontinent, religion still defines communities and cultures; and the Muslim conquests that began in the eleventh century have left a legacy of their own in architecture, with the Taj itself a world-famous example. In its use of the arch and the dome, the Muslim style reflects the styles of Persia; and its contribution is, relatively, a recent one.

India's ancient architectural tradition, closely bound up with religious faith, is older by many centuries than the Indo-Islamic one. Sanskrit treatises called the *Shilpa Shastras*, codified by A.D. 600, include material from a millennium earlier. They cover all aspects of art, and one text decrees that an architect "must be trained in music. . . . be a mathematician and historian. . . . be proficient in painting. . . . and must be above committing errors." He must also know the *Vedas*, the sacred lore passed down by brahmin priests. The *Vedas* preserve echoes of the time when Aryan tribes from Central Asia made their way into northern India, about 1500 B.C. Hymns salute the war god Indra as "breaker of cities."

No large-scale structures appear in the archaeological record for generations thereafter. Here and there mud-walled houses might vary the

PRECEDING PAGES: From peak to peak a mountain range of faith soars—entry porch, vestibule, and assembly hall rising toward the god Shiva's sanctum. Soaring fervor raised the Vishvanatha Temple a thousand years ago at Khajuraho, where it stands today in floodlit grandeur, a shrine of Hindu art.

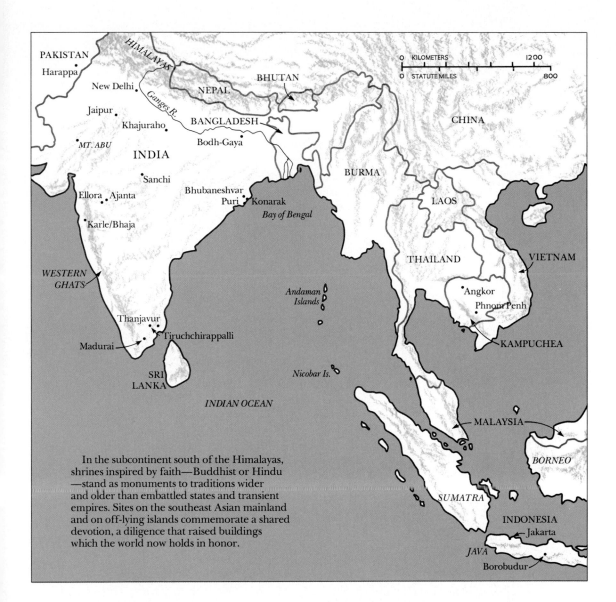

In the subcontinent south of the Himalayas, shrines inspired by faith—Buddhist or Hindu—stand as monuments to traditions wider and older than embattled states and transient empires. Sites on the southeast Asian mainland and on off-lying islands commemorate a shared devotion, a diligence that raised buildings which the world now holds in honor.

range of ephemeral huts of wood or bamboo and thatch. In time, with native and Aryan cultures blending in the north, a new pattern takes shape. Specialists think it included a developing art of timber architecture. By 800 B.C. iron was in use in many regions, for a variety of tools; bullocks and horses and elephants, long since domesticated, were at work; and settlements were growing into cities in the Ganges Plain and elsewhere.

Stone architecture—some of the earliest extant in South Asia—appeared with the growth of Buddhism, a faith that challenged the orthodoxy of brahmin priests. About 500 B.C. a prince named Siddhartha Gautama, distressed by the misery of the world, left his home at the foot of the Himalayas in search of truth and an end to mortal suffering. While meditating under a pipal tree at Bodh-Gaya, he gained insight and became the Buddha—the Enlightened One. When he preached his first sermon, he "set in motion the Wheel of the Law," teaching that pain and

sorrow stem from the very existence of desire. To attain release one must overcome desire by following the Buddha's path and his example.

When the Buddha died, his followers divided his cremated bodily relics and enshrined them in eight stupas, monuments patterned after the earthen burial mounds of local rulers.

Sometime around 260 B.C. King Ashoka of the Mauryan Dynasty, heir to the first empire that commanded most of the subcontinent, professed the ethics of Buddhism. He opened seven of the original stupas and divided the relics among 84,000 new ones—or so said Fa Xian, a Chinese pilgrim who marveled at Ashoka's works about seven centuries later.

A shrine founded by Ashoka, enlarged and embellished, stands almost perfectly preserved on a hill in central India. I first saw the Great Stupa at Sanchi after an all-night bus ride. Illumined by a saffron sunrise, its rounded dome seemed to float on the dark wooded crest like the cosmic egg that emerged from the primeval waters in Indian myth.

Typical of others in its time, the Great Stupa began as a mound perhaps 20 feet high and 60 feet in diameter, a hemisphere of kiln-burnt brick and mud mortar. In the second century B.C. builders virtually doubled its size by constructing a shell of hammer-dressed sandstone over a thick layer of rubble. On the summit a stone railing encloses a sacred pillar with a triple canopy stylized in stone.

At ground level a massive railing, 11 feet high, encircles the stupa. Built of stone, this balustrade was constructed as if in wood; broad crossbars fit into mortises cut in the posts. About a century later, great stone gateways called *toranas* were added. In design they resemble wooden prototypes; but the architraves, 20 feet wide, ride squarely on the upright members as befits heavy masonry. (A good 28 feet high without their crowning ornaments, Sanchi's toranas are 4 feet taller than the highest sarsen trilithon at Stonehenge.)

Outside and within the balustrade, worshipers would perform the rite called *pradakshina,* walking clockwise around a venerated object to pay reverence and draw inspiration. Thus Buddhism transformed a memorial to the dead into an aid to salvation for the living.

Richly carved with scenes illustrating Buddhist scripture and legend, the toranas imply a long development of timber architecture. They record in marvelous detail contemporary structures of wood and brick, long since vanished. Archers take aim from lofty battlements, chariots roll through grand gateways, and spectators look down on royal processions from arcaded balconies. Traces of a translucent red stain indicate that Sanchi's reliefs once glowed with color, as did royal palaces. Megasthenes, a Greek emissary to the Mauryan court, wrote a wide-eyed—and widely quoted—account of third-century B.C. India. The capital, he reported, was girded by a timber palisade crowned with 570 towers and pierced by

Buddhist compassion personified, a bodhisattva seems to bear the sorrows of a teeming world; the mural adorns a cave cut into the curving gorge at Ajanta.
FOLLOWING PAGES: Hewn from solid rock, the worship cave at Karle, c. A.D. 120, mimics wooden temples of a great architectural tradition almost entirely lost. Such vaulted ceilings rarely appear in later, freestanding stone structures.

64 gateways, and the palace boasted wooden pillars ornamented with designs of birds and foliage in gold and silver of great magnificence.

Over the centuries, as Buddhism flourished, brick-and-wood structures served the monastic centers at Sanchi and other sacred places: dormitories and refectories, preaching halls and libraries, rest houses for pilgrims. Meanwhile, some monks made the cave—a traditional shelter for Indian ascetics—the home of their communities. On the steep slopes of the mountain range called the Western Ghats, any structure might be at risk in the monsoon rains. Here, one scholar writes, the hills alone seemed secure: "With their great desire to make the Good Law of the Buddha outlast time itself," the monks "decided to carve their great sanctuaries out of the living rock of the immovable mountains."

In the thousand years after 150 B.C., more than a thousand caves were excavated in layered traprock. The rock-cut interiors served as *viharas,* living quarters with individual cells around a central chamber, and as *chaitya* halls, for worship. These man-made caves mimic features of timber structures: doorways crowned by arched gables and latticework; carved beams; barrel-vault ceilings. (The vaults suggest the sophistication of carpenters who probably joined short timbers into the graceful curves that later masons could not imitate in freestanding stone structures.)

Unfinished caves give an idea of the procedure. First, a natural escarpment was cut away to achieve a vertical face, on which the facade was blocked out. A hallmark of chapels was a large horseshoe-shaped opening above the entrance. Excavation began at the top of this arch; rock debris was removed through the cut as work progressed from front to back,

from the ceiling downward. Quarrymen made rough cuts with heavy picks. They had to avoid too deep a cut, for the margin for error was small. Close behind, stonecutters dressed the walls with hammers and chisels, probably using narrow iron blades for a fine-textured finish. Then other skilled artisans sculpted and painted—completing the task level by level, thus minimizing the need for scaffolding.

One of the oldest sites is Bhaja, where a score of caves were cut in a cliff near an ancient trade route. With a goatherd as guide, I climbed a steep path to a deserted terrace dominated by a great yawning archway. Sockets in the facade hint at timber attachments for a structure in wood.

Inside, I noticed struts and brackets chiseled in stone, and saw how the roof is "reinforced" with teak ribs thought to be original. The 27 octagonal pillars divide the hall into a nave and two side aisles; these form an ambulatory around a small rock-cut stupa, the focus of worship. In the shadowy depths of the chapel, the only sound was birdsong.

But as I emerged into the sunlight, that music was swelled by the chirruping of thirty-odd schoolchildren scrambling up the hillside. They swirled in and out of the chapel, running rings around pillars, playing hide-and-seek in niches, and trying out stone sleeping benches in nearby cells that had kept monks cool in summer and warm in winter two thousand years ago. They alighted long enough to gobble up puffed rice snacks and fill their canteens at a rock-cut cistern. Then, as teachers counted glossy black heads, the children fluttered back down the trail.

Grandest in scale of these caves is the chaitya hall at nearby Karle, its cavernous interior 124 feet in length and about 46 feet in both height and width. Its dark recesses evoke the cave of the mind, which the Enlightened One urged his followers to explore in his dying admonition: "Be a lamp unto yourselves."

At Ajanta, thirty caves, including five chaityas and two dozen viharas, were cut in a cliff by the Waghora River; and once murals adorned almost half of them. Walls were smoothed with plaster—mainly mud mixed with seeds, tiny pebbles, and pulverized pottery—and finished with a wash of lime. Possibly working by light reflected from outside by metal mirrors, artists used a palette of mineral colors ranging from yellow ocher through orange and red to dusky brown, as well as black and white, olive and forest green, and lustrous lapis lazuli. The few scenes that have survived the ravages of bats, bees, and beetles, rockfalls, smoke, damp, and restoration offer glimpses of life at royal courts in the fifth century. Dancing girls perform for their sovereign while a maid massages the queen's feet. A king sits cross-legged on an ivory throne as servants shower him with perfumed bathwater. An ascetic preaches to a rapt gathering. And a bodhisattva, one who postpones the bliss of nirvana to serve mankind, offers an image of serene compassion.

To the southwest, at Ellora, 34 major rock-cut sanctuaries punctuate a mile-long stretch of bluff. These belong to three traditions: Hinduism, Buddhism, and Jainism, a faith that flourished in the time of Prince Siddhartha. Unique among them is a Hindu temple dedicated to Shiva—not a cave but a monolith, a temple 164 feet long by 109 feet wide, rising 96 feet from the bottom of an immense quarry. Almost as wide as the Parthenon, 64 feet shorter but half again as high, it is spectacular in undertaking and achievement. *(Continued on page 140)*

135

The Great Stupa at Sanchi first arose in the third century B.C. *as a burnt-brick mound, enshrining a relic of the Buddha's body. Succeeding centuries saw the dome enlarged, encased in ashlar, or dressed stone (right), encircled by a walkway, adorned with gateways, crowned with a new three-tiered finial. Time has worn away a layer of concrete and plaster coating. Pious travelers spread both the message and the medium; the concept of the stupa influenced the styles of memorial structures across Asia, including the pagodas of China and Japan.* FOLLOWING PAGES: *In lotus position the Buddha sits amid pierced stupas of 1,200-year-old Borobodur in Java, a monument with twice the height and four times the area of Sanchi's Great Stupa.*

The excavation entailed removal of some 50,000 cubic yards of rock and may have taken a century. Artisans smoothed the outer walls of the deepening pit, carved the western side into a gateway, and chiseled the central hulk of stone into a complete temple: an entrance porch, a pavilion for Shiva's sacred bull; a colonnaded hall; five minor shrines around the sanctuary, the holy of holies. Everywhere, figures in high relief portray Shiva—Lord of the Dance, Slayer of Demons, Lord of Knowledge—and vivid hues of paint once brightened them.

Completed before A.D. 800, this Kailasanatha Temple marks the supreme achievement of rock-cut architecture in India. Moreover, it mimics not timber construction but masonry, for the Hindus' great age of temple building in stone was well under way.

Instead of arches and vaults, Indian masons relied on post-and-beam construction; they used stone lintels to span openings, and corbeling to cover interiors. With one stone seated solidly on another in horizontal courses, weight was transmitted straight downward, and builders rarely employed mortar, though on occasion they secured masonry with iron dowels at critical points. Cautiously, over centuries, architects added height to their towers. Around A.D. 1000, at Thanjavur (Tanjore) in the southeast, craftsmen succeeded in a daring venture: The pyramidal tower of the Brihadeshvara Temple still rises tier upon tier to a height of nearly 200 feet. This is topped by a domed capstone said to weigh 80 tons and to have been dragged to the summit up an earthen ramp several miles long.

In the south, rulers glorified their ancient shrines with encircling walls and gigantic brick-and-masonry *gopuras*, or gate towers. These grew more imposing from the twelfth century on. Late and florid examples are the gopuras at Madurai, which sweep up in a concave curve, bearing aloft images of the myriad gods and goddesses of the Hindu pantheon, all painted in gaudy colors.

In northern India the temple tower remained the dominant feature. It was called a *shikhara* (literally, in Sanskrit, a mountain peak). One scholar has compared its curves to those of a rustic shrine built of bamboo poles lashed together at the apex. To trace the development of the shikhara, I visited the state of Orissa, on the eastern coast. Here between A.D. 600 and 1300, ruling families contended with one another, showed some tolerance to subjects of other faiths, and built lavish temples for their own. At Bhubaneshvar alone, an ancient pilgrimage center, hundreds of temples were completed. Moreover, until 1568, Orissan rulers succeeded in staving off iconoclastic Muslim invaders who destroyed Hindu shrines elsewhere, and dozens of these temples survive. (Orissa is also a rich source of architectural texts, thanks to the custom of making a fresh copy of a palm-leaf manuscript every century or so and consigning the old one to the waters of a river.)

Small Hindu shrines dot the rice fields of the Orissan countryside, which had turned from monsoon green to harvest gold when I arrived in December. A bicycle rickshaw carried me among the temples at Bhubaneshvar, where many cluster near a sacred lake. At the seventh-century Parashurameshvara Temple I noted the squat, beehive-shaped *deul,* as

the sanctuary-and-tower unit is called in Orissa, and a porch roofed with sloping slabs of stone. This chamber where worshipers gaze into the shrine is a *jagamohana* (a Sanskrit term, referring to deity).

Loveliest of Bhubaneshvar's temples is the small, tenth-century Mukteshvara, with a deul only 33 feet high. Like all Hindu temples it is symbolic—as ancient texts explain—of Cosmic Man. The base is compared to the foot and shins; the trunk of the tower curves inward to a narrow "neck." The "head" consists of a melon-shaped disk called an *amalaka,* capped by a "skull" and crowned by a *kalasha,* or vase of immortality, with a sacred symbol as finial. The holiest inner shrine is the *garba-griha,* literally, the "womb house." Dark, cavelike, it focuses all attention on the object of the cult. This, in Shiva's temples, is the *lingam,* a phallic symbol, encircled by the *yoni,* or vulva; together they represent the creative energy of the universe. Reflecting cosmic order and complex mathematics, a sacred diagram called a *mandala* underlies the plan of the temple complex; often the fundamental form is the square, symbol of perfection and stability.

At the Mukteshvara, I passed from the dazzling morning sunlight through the half-light of the jagamohana with its stone-latticed windows, and into a dim narrow passage to obtain *darshan,* an auspicious glimpse of the sacred image. There, by the flickering light of oil lamps, a slim young priest wearing a cerise silk dhoti was garlanding the lingam with hibiscus and jasmine.

Quarries in nearby hills supplied sandstone for these temples; that of the Rajarani Temple is a beautiful blend of russet and gold. The stones are fitted so precisely that intricate carving carries seamlessly from one block to another. Like other Orissan temples, these bloom with symbols of abundance, such as vases overflowing with foliage and lions disgorging strands of pearls. Everywhere there are *alasa-kanyas,* "indolent maidens." A text nine centuries old declares: "As a house without a wife, as frolic without a woman, so without the figure of woman the monument will be of inferior quality and bear no fruit." The author describes in detail 16 types of ideal beauties, including a drummer and a dancer. Similarly, *mithunas,* or amorous couples, should adorn a temple, for "desire is the root of the universe. From desire all beings are born. . . . A place without love-images is. . . . a base, forsaken place."

The most exuberant display of love-images embellishes a group of shrines at Khajuraho, in central India. Here, according to local lore, the rulers built as many as 80 temples, both Hindu and Jain, in the tenth and eleventh centuries. About 25 temples still stand in fairly good condition, the finest with sculpture restored or intact.

Khajuraho's craftsmen dissolved the boundaries between sculpture and architecture to create a cosmic vision out of honey-hued sandstone. On all these temples, sharply etched cornices and friezes make dramatic play with brilliant sunlight and deep shadow. On the lowest or terrestrial

FOLLOWING PAGES: Bright, filmy saris warm the cool marble geometry of Tejapala Temple on Mount Abu, famed for its intricate carving. Built in the 13th century, this is the shrine of Neminatha, one of 24 holy teachers of Jainism who have conquered earthly passions and attained perfect knowledge.

Memories of a golden age crowd the abandoned temples of Khajuraho—a joyous cavalcade of gods and goddesses, warriors, animals, dancers, ravishing nymphs, couples in passionate embrace. In the tenth and eleventh centuries Chandella rajas endowed many temples here, of which a score remain. The sculptures, of fine-grained sandstone, range the human tableau: People toy with pets, yawn, scratch. The woman at left pokes at her foot—perhaps pulling a thorn, perhaps coating the sole with henna, as custom decreed. Sexual scenes abound, a human semblance of divine creative forces, hinting at joys transcending the sensual. The lofty Vishvanatha tower (right), enshrines a lingam, *a stylized phallus representing the creative power of the god Shiva.*

level, carvings depict armies on the march, laborers at work, hunters and their quarry. On the celestial level, outside the shrine, deities and their consorts, with hosts of heavenly nymphs and their lovers, pose and posture, embrace and entwine. Through the highest zone, the roofs of the antechambers rise in crescendo to the shikhara, the pinnacle of the universe. The profile of the 100-foot spire of the Kandariya Mahadeva Temple is repeated by 84 lesser shikharas superimposed on the core of the cosmic mountain—architecture by accumulation.

Here the Jain shrines resemble the Hindu temples in form and iconography. But to the west, at a village called Dilwara, ornament eclipses architecture in the five Jain temples. According to local lore, their white Makrana marble was hauled by elephants up the weary slopes of Mount Abu. The exterior of the Vimala Temple is as ascetic as the Jain faith. But to step inside is to enter a crystalline world as intricate and fragile as a snowflake. This marble filigree, says tradition, was achieved not with a sculptor's chisel but with the delicate file of a jeweler, and craftsmen were paid by the weight of the filings.

In vivid contrast, sheer massiveness distinguishes three monumental structures that mark a climax of temple building in Orissa: the Lingaraja Temple in Bhubaneshvar, the Jagannatha Temple in Puri, and the Sun Temple at Konarak. The Lingaraja complex, said to have enjoyed continual use for nearly a millennium, encompasses more than a hundred shrines. Two added structures show the elaboration of ritual: a hall for music and dancing, and a hall of offerings, where donations of foodstuffs were received and portions of *prasad,* or consecrated food, were distributed to devotees.

At Puri, on the coast, the temple of Jagannatha (sometimes considered an aspect of Vishnu) has been a magnet for pilgrims at least since the twelfth century and possibly much longer. At the onset of the monsoon, I went to Puri—with 600,000 other people— *(Continued on page 151)*

Weathered workhorse of deity stands harnessed and caparisoned, ready to haul the chariot-temple of the sun across the skies. Seven centuries have left but a fragment of the Sun Temple built by a Hindu ruler in honor of his victories in battle. Here at Konarak are seven stone steeds, with 24 giant, elaborately carved chariot wheels. The tall sanctuary tower, crumbled now, oriented European sailors on the Bay of Bengal; they knew it as the Black Pagoda, in contrast to the White Pagoda, which still stands 20 miles up the coast at Puri. With joy Hindus welcomed the coming of Surya, the sun god, a daily procession that rekindled the heavens with light. Hindu believers still worship the sun, and festival processions, with images of deities carted about, mark the highlights of the Hindu year.
FOLLOWING PAGES: From the White Pagoda come images set in colorful rathas—chariots—for the car festival at Puri, attended by hundreds of thousands each summer. Worshipers on the ropes pull rathas bearing the Lord Jagannatha and three associated deities. From grisly tales of devotees crushed by the wheels in the Jagannatha procession came the word "juggernaut."

JOYCE STEWART (FOLLOWING PAGES)

to celebrate the *Ratha Yatra,* or Journey of the Chariots. Wooden images of Lord Jagannatha and three other deities are taken from the sanctum, placed on three heavy vehicles, and paraded on the main thoroughfare. There people of all castes (as well as non-Hindus, who are barred from the temple) can see them, make offerings, even touch them.

The day before the festival, the Maharaja of Puri, an elegant but unassuming young lawyer who inherited his title in 1970, explained his role in it. We were sipping coconut milk in his residence, surrounded by big game trophies shot by his grandfather. "Those are relics of the past, like my title, which confers on me no official standing in democratic India. But in accord with the people's wishes, I continue to perform various religious duties. Chief among them is the sweeping of the deities' chariots with a gold-handled broom before the start of the procession. I've missed this ceremony only once—when my law exams at Northwestern University in Chicago coincided with the festival—but I appointed a deputy, for tradition holds that the cars *must* be properly swept."

(The Chinese pilgrim Fa Xian described a similar procession by Buddhist monks around A.D. 400: ". . . they make a four-wheeled image-car about thirty feet high, in appearance like a moving palace. . . . They fix upon it streamers of silk and canopy curtains." Around the sacred images, he wrote, "all kinds of polished ornaments made of gold and silver hang suspended in the air." Fa Xian reported that the king went barefoot to meet the chariot and scatter flowers before it, and the queen and her ladies welcomed it with flowers tossed from the tower of the city gate: "So splendid are the arrangements for worship.")

I judged the chariots I saw to be more than 40 feet high, and they had 16, 14, and 12 wheels, respectively. Brilliant bunting covered their superstructures, which were shaped like the temple's shikhara. To the beat of gongs, priests broke coconuts over the wheels, and thousands of surging pilgrims seized hawsers to pull the ponderous chariots down the procession route with surprising swiftness—their task made light by the fervor of their devotion.

Twenty miles northeast along the coast, seven stone horses leap forward—"celestial coursers, revelling in their strength," in the imagery of the *Vedas*—straining to pull a colossal stone chariot into the sky. These are remnants of the most ambitious effort of Orissa's builders, the Sun Temple of Konarak, planned as the vehicle in which Surya, "sun god with hair of flame," makes his celestial journey.

In the mid-13th century Prince Narasimha Deva I commissioned it. He planned a mighty 24-wheeled "chariot"—consisting of a vast assembly hall and a soaring tower—and a separate festival hall. That hall is now a roofless pavilion. To forestall collapse of the jagamohana, it was buttressed inside and filled with sand in 1905. The tower is but a stump and

In rituals of morning, Hindu worshipers greet the new day with puja, *a rite of honor and devotion. Beside the tank rises tenth-century Mukteshvara Temple, one of many ancient shrines still standing in the holy city of Bhubaneshvar. The steep-sided sanctum holds a symbol of Shiva; the pyramidal roof of the porch bears the style of Orissa, once a land of rival kings, today a state of the Indian Union.*

Body language thaws the cold stone of temple carvings, transmuting the frozen stances into the lyric flow of traditional dance (right). A member of the Orissa dance academy takes position at the Mukteshvara Temple gateway; every movement—even of an eyebrow—has meaning in the choreography of myth and scripture. Architects in Orissa drew on Sanskrit, the ancient classical language, for terms of human anatomy—trunk, neck, head—and applied these to parts of their temple towers. On the "head" appears the ribbed feature called an amalaka, obscure in symbolism but striking in effect, as on the Lingaraja Temple at Bhubaneshvar (left).

the sanctum stands vacant and open to the sky. Yet the Sun Temple remains one of the most awe-inspiring of monuments.

The proportions are elegant, the sculptures superb, in a coarse-grained gneiss the color of old coral. On the roof of the jagamohana, dancers larger than life, playing cymbals and drums, speed Surya's chariot with music. And huge entrance guardians—rampant lions, rearing stallions, enraged elephants—trumpet the might of a dynasty that could boast of warriors and war horses and war elephants by the thousand.

Why was so grand a temple built in an isolated delta? Where did the stone come from? Where were the artisans and artists found? Could it have been completed in a dozen years, as legend says? Was it ever really finished? And why did the tower collapse? Experts have long debated such questions.

Some answers have come from palm-leaf manuscripts, discovered in local villages by a scholar from Puri, carefully translated, and published in 1972. These documents include elegant drawings of structures now lost, notes on symbolism (such as the fact that each pair of stone wheels was dedicated to one of the signs of the zodiac), and a handbook of ritual. Especially valuable is a book of accounts, which tells of materials, work force, and costs in great detail.

Now separated from the sea by nearly two miles of sand, the temple once stood on the shore where it caught dawn's first rays—or so it is said. Artisans were recruited throughout the region. Local communities volunteered goods and labor, and neighboring rulers sent gifts: 50 "pairs of cloth" from one raja, 5 cartloads of raw-iron lumps from another, 2,304 60-foot timbers from a local chief. The prince's father-in-law sent ten *shilpis,* architect-sculptors, from Madurai. The workers were housed in camps and paid in money, in kind (including rice, oil and clarified butter), or in land, as were cooks and sweepers, torchlighters and latrine cleaners, even an informer "for finding out what was being talked at night."

The prince made Sadashiva Samantaraya Mahapatra his "holder of the thread," or chief architect. His principal lieutenants included a superintendent of works, a head stonemason, and a chief image-maker. Under them were the 700 shilpis. Also, ordinary and specialist stonecutters, carpenters and ironworkers, boatmen and drivers of bullock carts. Women were hired to pound limestone, and to make bamboo pegs; one was a sculptress; three small elephants and 37 women with heavy wooden pestles leveled the floor in the jagamohana. Elephants also pulled sand plows to clear away drifts, and helped dig a canal to the site.

Many jobs were subcontracted. A carpenter was paid in gold (232 coins called *madha*) for delivery of 483 pointed chisels, 326 indented chisels, 130 flat chisels, 308 mallets, 47 wooden plates with a hole for passing a plumb line, and a right-angled measuring rod. When the chief architect declared the Madurai sculptors' work unacceptable—probably because of the distinctive Madurai style—they went on a hunger strike. The prince, loath to offend his father-in-law, tactfully suggested that they be set to carving ornamental details such as vines.

Workers spent months at quarries, some more than 100 miles distant. Stones were brought by barge and raft on inland waterways. (One raft sank during a cyclone; a diver and three elephants were hired to retrieve the cargo.) Tallymen counted the stones on arrival, and—to speed the project—workmen laid out the stones in the order of their use. Elaborate timber scaffolding was erected (earthen ramps, incidentally, are never mentioned). Stones were wheeled on dollies; carried slung from shoulder poles; hoisted in rope nets. Lifting systems used cranes, pulleys, winches, and elephant-powered levers. An on-site foundry made iron cramps and dowels, and iron girders to reinforce ceilings.

Working at times by torchlight, and through the monsoon season (when work was usually halted), the builders completed the temple in time for an initial rite of worship on an auspicious spring day in 1258. The keeper of accounts noted in closing the books that the records had covered 12 years, 10 months, and 14 days, and added that "my black hair has become white."

By this happy season the prince had succeeded his father as maharaja, and the cost of the temple, it is said, was a thousand times Narasimha's weight in gold. But its fame spread afar; and when the Mogul court chronicler of the Emperor Akbar visited the Sun Temple around the year 1580, he declared that "even those whose judgment is critical and who are difficult to please stand astonished at its sight."

Half a century later the Sun Temple had begun to crumble. One tale says that during a Muslim invasion the gilded kalasha was removed from the top of the tower, thus exposing plaster which the rains slowly washed away. Scholars suspect that the caretakers had been negligent with repairs, and that the rush to finish the structure may have left hidden flaws. Perhaps the iron cramps of the ponderous amalaka stones rusted and gave way, and the stones began to move. The balance of the spire was lost, and with it stability. When a tower wall collapsed, reports a chronicle, "the entire country fell into great affliction."

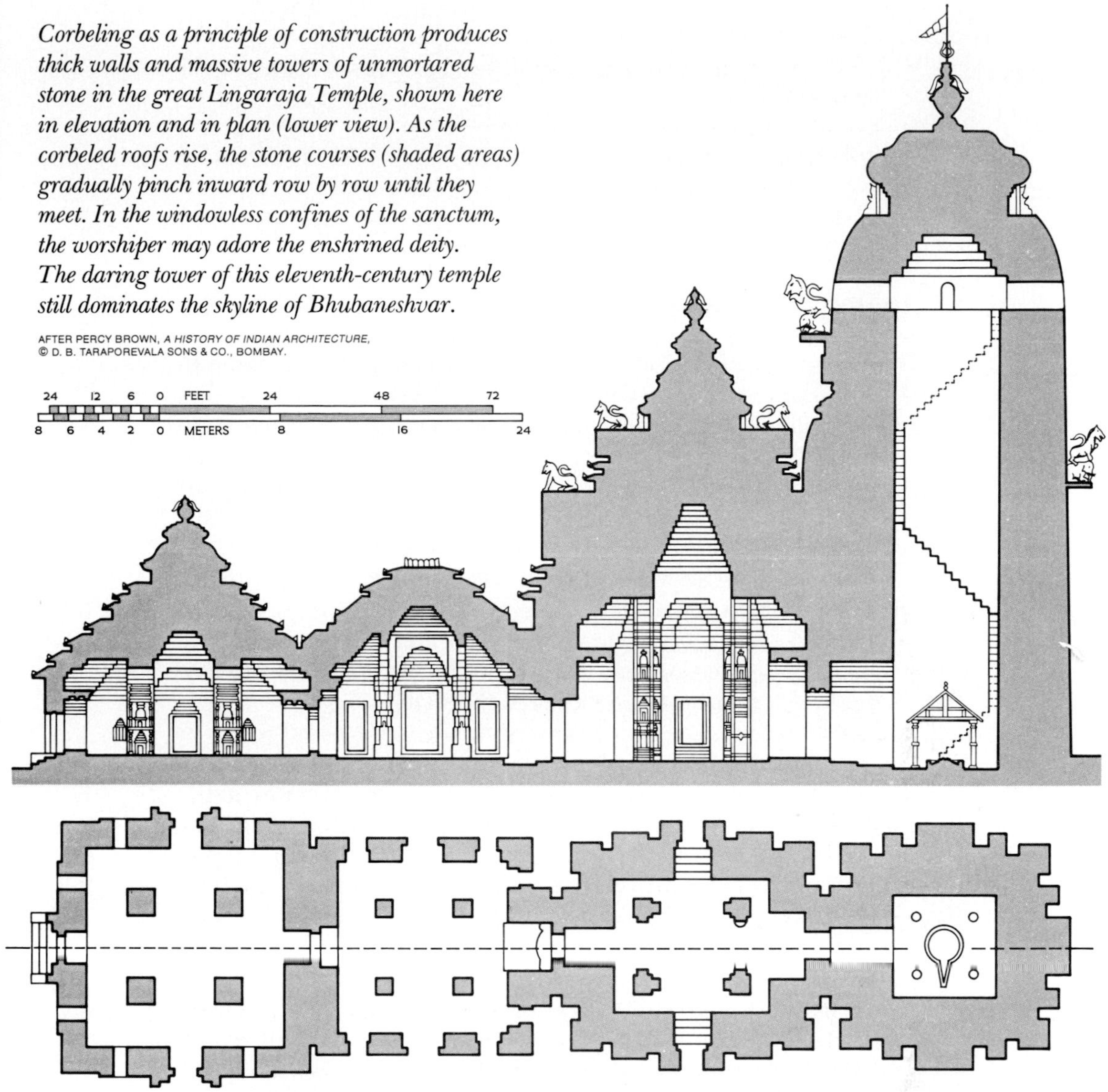

Corbeling as a principle of construction produces thick walls and massive towers of unmortared stone in the great Lingaraja Temple, shown here in elevation and in plan (lower view). As the corbeled roofs rise, the stone courses (shaded areas) gradually pinch inward row by row until they meet. In the windowless confines of the sanctum, the worshiper may adore the enshrined deity. The daring tower of this eleventh-century temple still dominates the skyline of Bhubaneshvar.

AFTER PERCY BROWN, *A HISTORY OF INDIAN ARCHITECTURE,*
© D. B. TARAPOREVALA SONS & CO., BOMBAY.

Outside the subcontinent, however, spectacular monuments had brought splendor and consolation as religions of Indian origin spread to the high, cold deserts of Central Asia; to the humid plains of Southeast Asia; to the volcanic islands of the Indonesian archipelago.

As monks and traders carried Buddhism over caravan routes, stupas grew taller and more ornate. In the second century A.D., a stupa near modern Peshawar became a wonder of the Buddhist world. According to a sixth-century Chinese pilgrim, its top rose an astounding 700 feet above ground level (145 feet higher, that is, than the Washington Monument).

In central Java, encasing and crowning a hill on the fertile Kedu Plain, builders completed a colossal Buddhist monument some years after A.D. 800. This is Borobudur, a structure of unmortared stones with a base 403 feet square and a height of 105 feet; its terraces take the visitor on a symbolic ascent to freedom from the bondage of mortal existence. It was

rescued from ruin by an international reconstruction project completed in 1982. Two of the project's consultants discussed it with me recently when I visited the site.

Dr. Parmono Atmadi, a professor of architecture, summarized three major problems that plagued his forebears: "Uncompacted fill caused subsidence. The original design exerted too much outward thrust for the base. And, most damaging over time, water seepage not only aggravated the structural instability but led to corrosion of the stone." And architect Jacques Dumarçay told me why the structure had bulged and buckled but held together despite earthquakes, volcanic eruptions, and abandonment for centuries: "As stones shifted, right-angle joints locked all the more firmly. Masons had also linked blocks with tenons and mortises, and with double-dovetailed stone clamps." Other ingenious devices had supplied strength, as skillfully as the splendid carvings had imparted the teachings of the Enlightened One.

Marvels of architecture, both Hindu and Buddhist, and elaborate systems of hydraulic engineering distinguished Angkor, a capital of the Khmer Empire that ruled in Southeast Asia a thousand years ago. Greatest of its "temple-mountains" is the world-famous Angkor Wat, a shrine to Vishnu, a byword for size and sumptuous ornament.

But construction on this scale always taxes human ingenuity, and Khmer techniques often proved unsound. Builders embedded laterite slabs in sand-filled trenches to provide level foundations for their mortarless sandstone edifices; when water seeped in, the sand shifted under its burden and the structure settled—unevenly. To reinforce a structure, eleventh-century carpenters concealed wooden beams in hollowed-out stone blocks; when the wood rotted, the masonry collapsed.

Here as elsewhere, however, works of art retain their ancient eloquence. From 49 towers on the immense Buddhist shrine called the Bayon, huge faces suggest the majesty of supernatural guardians. Unique in Buddhist art, they preserve its imagery of compassion, just as the exuberant figures of Khajuraho express celestial delights.

Construction of stupas and temples embodying these cosmic themes engaged the energies of thousands of artisans and answered the aspirations of millions of worshipers between the third century B.C. and the thirteenth century A.D.—and afterward. Under the creative impetus of faith, giving concrete expression to complex belief, builders relied on the simplest of principles—basically, one stone laid upon another, bound together by the forces of gravity—to produce spectacular architecture. In compass, quantity, and sustained vitality, their accomplishment is as great as, or greater than, any the world has ever seen.

South India's distinctive architectural form, the giant gateways called gopuras *mark the walls surrounding ancient temples—often modest, always most holy—such as the Shrirangam Temple at Tiruchchirappalli. Bamboo, the traditional scaffolding, sheathes a gopura where workmen restore the sacred images.*
FOLLOWING PAGES: Guardian faces gentle the pocked stone of the Bayon at Angkor, carved in obedience to the orders of a Buddhist king. From India man-made mountains of faith had spread to the land of the Khmer.

WILBUR E. GARRETT, N.G.S. STAFF (FOLLOWING PAGES)

CHINA

CHINA

By Ann Nottingham Kelsall
Photographs by National Geographic Photographer Dean Conger

Confidently astride an imaginary horse, a small boy galloped cheerfully through the quiet halls of the Chinese History Museum in Beijing. The sound of his heels clattered incongruously through the solemn marble corridors full of display cases bidding unsuccessfully for his attention. Suddenly he stopped. *"Ai ya!"* he gasped. He had been startled by a dark tower, considerably taller than he, firmly set in his path. His eyes widened with curiosity as he studied its tiny balconies, each punctuated by silent windbells and supported by a maze of wooden brackets as intricate as clockwork. With a smile he raised his hand in salute to a jovial monk grinning down at him from a doorway just a bit above the level of his nose.

We were in Gallery Six, which is devoted to the builders of the Song Dynasty in China and its "barbarian" neighbors to the north. The display that so captured the youngster's attention is a reproduction in meticulous miniature of the great pagoda at Yingxian in northern Shanxi Province. The original, built in A.D. 1056, still stands in the arid plains not far from the ancient city of Datong. An architectural tour de force, constructed entirely of wood, it stands in proud tribute to traditional Chinese craftsmanship and the ancient carpenter's art.

Because I had recently returned from Shanxi Province myself, the child's excitement recalled my own when I first saw that majestic silhouette, its wondrous detail etched against a pale yellow sky.

In Gallery Six, I was also reminded that timber-frame construction is only one elegant example of the ingenuity of ancient engineers and craftsmen who gave shape to the ideas that governed the Chinese world. Near me hung a 13th-century map of Suzhou. The plan, a rubbing taken from a stele, clearly shows a well-planned city. On a platform a few yards distant, a model of a water-driven astronomical clock tower evokes Chinese scientific achievements as of A.D. 1088. In one corner of the gallery stands a model of a Song iron foundry. Each of these exhibits dramatizes the persistence of a long technological tradition and a mature civilization—a people confident of their placc in the center of the world.

By the time the Yingxian pagoda was built, Song Dynasty scholars looked back with awe at the work of the ancients a thousand years earlier. They also admired the empires of the more recent past, yet they were conscious of living in a different world. The Great Wall no longer protected the Middle Kingdom from northern invaders; descendants of nomads occupied much of the land north of the Yellow River. Chang'an, capital

PRECEDING PAGES: Bold and graceful at once, the style of the Song Dynasty (A.D. 960-1279) survives in a pavilion of the Jin temple complex near Taiyuan in northern China. Regional idiom supplied the round windows. Here, on the Water Mirror Terrace, musicians, actors, and poets have performed for centuries.

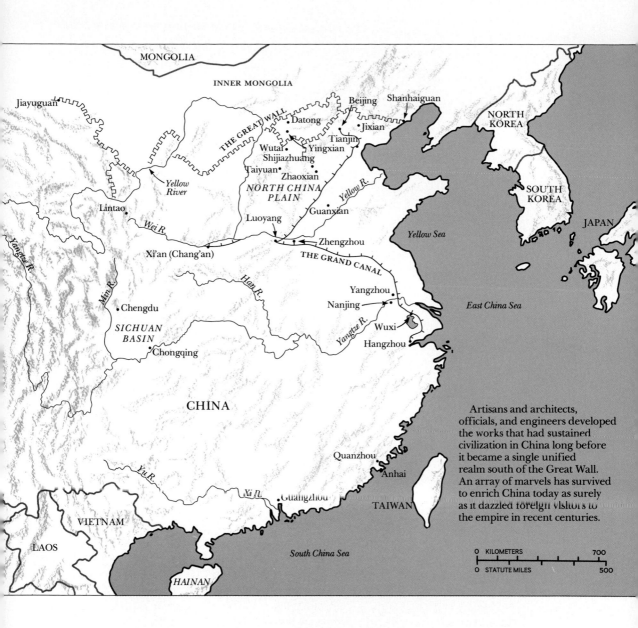

Artisans and architects, officials, and engineers developed the works that had sustained civilization in China long before it became a single unified realm south of the Great Wall. An array of marvels has survived to enrich China today as surely as it dazzled foreign visitors to the empire in recent centuries.

city of the Han and Tang Dynasties, had long since been looted and destroyed. "China" was a smaller place now, and much of its population had migrated southward in flight from northern aggressors.

In the 11th and 12th centuries A.D., Song China's capital cities, first at Kaifeng and later Hangzhou, each in turn became more populous and far richer than any of their contemporaries anywhere. Their populations became increasingly dependent on traditional engineering skills to support an expanding commercial economy. To the north, China's rivals (who in Chinese fashion styled themselves the Liao Dynasty) supervised construction of many great temples and towers. Among these was the wooden pagoda at Yingxian, built according to well-established standards accepted as valid by "barbarian" and Chinese alike.

Viewed from a distance, the great pagoda gives an impression of weight and solidity. Unlike some of its graceful stone cousins in the south,

which seem about to float on the wind, this massive tower remains planted resolutely on the ground. A tribute to its builders, given the nature of the place—I vividly remember my last day in Shanxi Province.

In order to keep my eyes open, I had to turn my back to the wind. It had been driving all day; I had sand in my hair and grit in my teeth. My Chinese companions hardly seemed to notice the storm. The spring winds have been thrumming over this land for centuries, carrying with them layer after layer of fine yellow dust.

This region, northeast of the great bend of the Yellow River, is part of China's great loess plateau. The loess, a fine silt from the Gobi, is deposited continually over the broad reaches of the river valley. There it compacts itself into golden moonscapes raked with gullies and gorges, or piles itself into hillsides hundreds of feet high. It makes an airy topsoil, both fertile and friable; but in its natural state it shifts or collapses easily. For millennia the Chinese have been plowing it, digging it, planting it, pounding it. Properly treated, loess is a natural building material. Hollowed out, it makes cool caves; shaped into neat dwellings, it shelters whole villages; but above all, loess, rammed and pounded, is the stuff of walls.

I n countryside where villages, terraces, and fields all seem to meld into the hills that enclose them, pounded-earth walls are ordinary things. So common that they have been called synonymous with Chinese civilization, they have been standing steel-hard, some of them for thousands of years. New ones take shape today alongside their traditional fellows, products of extraordinary effort.

By tradition, construction began on a carefully prepared foundation, usually of rubble stone. To give the wall its form, timber or bamboo frames provided support. Little by little, workers poured in thin layers of soil, adding more only after each layer was beaten hard. In ancient times the din of wooden mallets rang through the air for weeks and months as a wall rose centimeter by centimeter. By such process an earthen wall two feet thick could rise ten feet or more (defensive walls much higher and thicker) and stand against the elements for centuries.

I had visited Datong partly to pay my respects to the most heroic of all Chinese walls, the Great Wall itself. I had already seen it, elegantly reconstructed, in the passes near Beijing and at Shanhaiguan, but I wanted to visit a place a little quieter. North of Datong only an occasional telegraph pole brings the look of modern things to the landscape.

Our Toyota left the highway just short of the Inner Mongolian border, and our driver deftly picked his way over unpaved ruts, and among startled villagers. He stopped at the edge of the Yu River, here a sizable stream. Somehow we had missed connections with the horse cart we expected to meet us, and we had to get across on foot.

It had been a dry spring and the water was low. My companion, Xiao Wang, leaped gracefully from stone to slippery stone. I took the safer course and, to the amusement of assembled villagers, waded in. The water, clear and clean, was cold as it filled my shoes.

Once across, we followed a well-beaten pathway, leaving the village behind. Slowly the outlines of signal towers emerged from the surrounding hills. In the shadowless sunshine they rose, pitted and brown like massive

166

cones of brown sugar. Between them the wall undulated gently as though some cosmic hand had shaped it between thumb and forefinger.

Then we made our way up the sloping side of the ancient barrier. In the near distance, somewhat obscured by dust, we could just make out the edges of a cluster of houses on the northern side, in Mongolia: Ten Towers Village, we later learned, built of brick and stone scavenged from the wall itself. Near it tiny dark figures moved through carefully tended fields, past neat rows just beginning to show a bright yellow-green. Children caught sight of us and shouted with excitement—the only sound to pierce the afternoon wind. Beneath us, on the southern side, a crude dwelling huddled, almost invisible, against the base of a silent watchtower.

Today's wall winds and stretches for about 2,500 miles (10,000 *li*, the Chinese love to say) from the coast near Shanhaiguan to the deserts of Gansu Province. There has been such a wall for nearly 2,000 years, but almost none of what we see now is original. The first wall, most of it constructed in the third century B.C., apparently traced a different course.

In fact the Great Wall has been many walls, built and rebuilt over time, but as a symbol of unity it has come to be associated with China's first empire and its legendary ruler Qin Shihuang, the Tiger of Qin. Records from the first century B.C. say that after Qin troops had forcibly united the warring kingdoms of the Yellow and Yangtze River valleys, their triumphant emperor ordered his trusted General Meng Tian to secure the northern frontier. General Meng, with at least 300,000 men at his command, did not have to start from scratch. Beginning with the fortifications that shielded several of the former kingdoms, he strengthened, extended, and connected them into one. This barrier ran considerably north of the line selected in later centuries. The most extensive building project ever undertaken, this zigzag wall would equal one-tenth of the earth's circumference, and it changed the face of Asia forever.

How was such a project undertaken? Did armies of laborers simply march out and start to work? Not at all.

Those arid regions along the northern border were sparsely populated, remote, difficult to provision. Building the wall required building entire communities to support the undertaking. At points along the frontier, battalions of laborers dug irrigation works, plowed new fields, built shelters and forts. In saline swamp country, wagon trains were organized to bring in grain. Only then could the real work begin.

Apparently the elegant monuments preserved today near Beijing or Shanhaiguan bear little resemblance to their remote ancestor of the third century B.C. General Meng's ragtag laborers, using whatever material they could get, strengthened and reinforced the wall with stone, bamboo, lumber, sand, pebbles—depending on local conditions. Thousands of

---

PRECEDING PAGES: Watchtowers keep vigil above China's Great Wall, begun in the third century B.C. as a barrier to marauding horsemen. Successive generations extended and restored it; eventually it stretched some 2,500 miles, from the Yellow Sea to the desert interior. FOLLOWING PAGES: Work on the wall continues today near Shanhaiguan, where laborers clear ancient foundations. Rammed earth fills the space between brick walls; projecting drains dispose of rainwater.

fortified watchtowers guarded strategic points and allowed a ready flow of signals. The Qin ramparts, if not so splendid as the work of later generations, effectively protected the new empire for several centuries from horseback raiders, and the peaceful movement of peoples across the frontier was monitored at gates provided for the purpose.

So great a feat was accomplished only at great cost. A Han Dynasty court historian, a century later, recorded: "He exposed his armies to the hardships of the frontier, never keeping less than twenty or thirty thousand in the field until the dead reached incalculable numbers, the corpses lay strewn for a thousand *li,* and streams of blood soaked the plains."

Tradition preserves the memory of millions who labored under the whip in the songs associated with Meng Jiang Nu—Lady Meng. Her husband was conscripted and sent to labor on a remote section of the eastern wall. With the onset of winter, so the legend goes, Lady Meng trekked over perilous miles to take him warm clothing. She arrived only to learn that her husband had already died of exhaustion. Then her tears flowed day after day until they undermined the foundations of the wall itself, causing it to crumble and leave a gap that remains to this day.

Moreover, tradition says that General Meng Tian paid for his cruelty—that he preferred suicide to execution, and died confessing that he had offended the cosmos itself by cutting through the veins of the earth, tampering with natural forces best left undisturbed.

Unfinished in the lifetime of the first emperor, the wall challenged the resources of the Han Dynasty, under whose aegis it was first completed. As the strength of succeeding dynasties varied, so did imperial attention to the northern border. Millions of hands had been required to build the wall, millions more to keep it in repair. Its success depended on continuous manning and diligent repair, neither of which it enjoyed consistently.

North of Datong there has been a wall at least since A.D. 607, when a million men were mobilized to complete a section between that city and Beijing. Records say that they did so in just twenty days. The most recent massive reconstruction came in the 15th century, when Ming emperors revamped the Great Wall's entire length. Remnants of that work lie crumbling along the border today.

The Ming wall was battered: That is, its outer faces sloped inward as they rose. A typical section of the eastern wall stood 20 or 30 feet high and measured 25 feet thick at the base, 15 across the top. At intervals of about a mile or so along its entire length, 1,700 watchtowers provided surveillance. Terrain permitting, the barrier was enhanced by a moat.

Even so, it was vulnerable. The section near Datong was breached on many occasions. During the eleventh century the kingdom founded by descendants of nomadic invaders actually straddled the great barrier.

Yet in spite of its failures, and its cost in human suffering, the Great

Buddhist prayer beads in hand, a smiling Mongolian monk greets visitors to Pusading Monastery at Wutai Shan, an ancient place of pilgrimage in Shanxi Province. Spreading into China from the first century A.D., Buddhism added the obligation of kindness to strangers to the Confucian ideals of loyalty to ruler, family, and friends. FOLLOWING PAGES: Chanting monks circle a temple courtyard.

Simplicity of form distinguishes the 800-year-old An Ping Bridge between villages by an estuary on China's southern coast. New guardrails follow the gentle curves of its course, here exaggerated by a telephoto lens. Longest of many ancient masonry structures, it runs almost a mile with some 360 piers like the one at right, each shaped to withstand the assault of currents. Granite beams, some 15 feet long, support the granite deck. Other ancient spans had slabs of 60 to 70 feet, of 150 to 200 tons apiece. To put these in place, builders used rafts and took advantage of the highest tides in spring and autumn.

Wall has always been a source of special pride for the Chinese. Once it was a boundary between inner and outer worlds—describing the perimeter of civilization itself. And within that boundary lay wonders.

"Ma che lu!" my guide Men Shifu grumbled good-naturedly, and he was right—the muddy road was fit only for horse carts. But I detected not a trace of sarcasm in Mr. Men's voice as he hailed a youngster nearby, "Please tell me, child, can you direct us to the Great Luminous Palace?"

The little boy pointed solemnly to a stone tablet just down the road: Here was the southeastern limit of the palace complex, the *Da Ming Gong*. This unpretentious neighborhood in modern Xi'an was once the most exalted section of Chang'an, grand imperial capital of the Tang Dynasty. This was a place full of ghosts. We were standing on an elevation known in the ninth century as Dragon Head Plain. Stately parades of dignitaries once glided along its thoroughfares. On days of sufficient solemnity they might have turned north to the glistening white Hall Embracing the Beginning to prostrate themselves before the throne. There the emperor sat—at the center of the world, the pivot upon which the earth turned.

Today, little remains visible. "Nothing is out there! Don't bother!" Often that was the answer to my questions about the Great Luminous Palace. But this is the place that inspired the architects of the Forbidden City in Beijing and the great temples of Nara, Japan. It did not disappoint me.

As I approached a colossal rectangular platform where one of the principal palaces had stood, I came under the gaze of grinning dragon faces, their chins pressed against the weeds growing out of the pounded earth. On the platform were arrays of stone disks. Mr. Zhu, the official in charge of preservation, explained: "They are pillar bases, copies of the originals which lie buried underneath. These treasures, once excavated, are far too precious to leave lying about. We rebury them, and place a model above

175

ground so people can see what has been discovered." He showed me about with much gesticulation: "Here a great door once swung. There in that stone basin, it is said, Yang Gui-fei [the beloved concubine] once bathed. And out there—beyond that village—beyond that row of trees— you can just make out the shadow of the *next* mound." I began to grasp the sheer scale of the place, and the care with which it is tended.

For the Chinese, their ruler was the Son of Heaven and his capital needed to reflect the order of the Universe. Therefore the art of building was too important to be left to human invention. Along with writing, music, and the rules of etiquette, knowledge of such things was a gift from the gods themselves. According to one myth, Fu Xi—the cosmic creator, who along with his sister put primal chaos in order—brandished a builder's square as symbol of his authority; and the divine hero Gun, the First Engineer, taught people to build the first walled cities.

China's oldest arched stone bridge leaps the Jiao River at Zhaoxian in the northern province of Hebei. Master builder Li Chun erected it about A.D. 610, brilliantly meeting the technical challenge of designing a flattened (or segmented) arch that would not collapse in the middle. Twin openings at each end of the 115-foot span lessen the weight of masonry to be supported, and also provide spillways for floodwaters. "How lofty is the flying arch! How large is the opening, yet without piers!" marveled a visiting official about 675. Anji Bridge has attracted travelers from the first. Their accounts spread its fame, and other builders copied its graceful form. Marco Polo reported the technique when he returned from China to Italy in 1295; apparently his account inspired European engineers in Florence, Venice, and other cities.

The earth, to the ancient Chinese, was an organic thing. Like a human body it had flesh, bones, and veins. In the earth and in every object, *chi*—energy—flowed through divine conduits. In his every act the Chinese builder felt called upon to respect this divine anatomy. To do otherwise would be to court disaster. For a garden wall or a royal palace, builders consulted geomancers, specialists in this sacred lore, for advice on selecting a site. The geomancers took careful measurements of sunlight and shade, the direction of running water, and the lay of the land in general, to determine whence evil spirits might propel gale, flood, or other perils.

Winter was the time for work, when hands otherwise occupied with farming would be available. A city's walls, the residence of its guardian spirits, were built first. Hammers pounded to a rhythm paced by the thunder of a drum. Laborers sang as they worked. Foremen hovered near lest any malcontent bring bad luck by uttering inauspicious verses.

Gates, at least one on each side, were built with special care, while multistory watchtowers provided warning against invaders. Walls complete, workers prepared an altar to the gods of the soil, and next an ancestral temple. Only then was it appropriate to construct residential and official quarters for the ruler and his minions. The administrative district, laid out on a north-south axis, occupied the city's center; the chief magistrate ruled there as did the Son of Heaven, seated on a dais facing south.

According to accepted wisdom, Heaven was round and the earth was square. The ideal configuration of a new city was a rectangle, its walls aligned with the four cardinal directions.

The ideal configuration was just that: an ideal. Frequently violated. Rectangles swelled into circles, squeezed into trapezoids, or bulged into amoeboid globs as the terrain demanded. The gods, it seems, condoned the exercise of common sense. Even in Chang'an, the ideal was less than sacrosanct. In 662 the emperor decided to move from his central palace complex to the Dragon Head Plain—because, said some, he thought its slightly higher elevation better for his rheumatism.

Whether or not Chang'an conformed to cosmic specifications, the Chinese still prize the memory of its glory. In the eighth century it was home to at least a million people; its tree-lined boulevards welcomed traders, monks, and adventurers from points as distant as Malacca or Calicut. Muslims, Christians, and Buddhists mingled in its markets, opened daily to the din of 300 drums. One hundred and ten residential wards enjoyed such urban amenities as heroic sewer systems. Goods reached the metropolis by way of canals. But the fabled city fell in 907, victim of poor management, economic reverses, and internal rebellion, and little remained of its palaces but dust.

No Chinese city ever again approached its majesty, but each in turn paid tribute to its spirit. Today, visitors in Beijing leave the Forbidden City through the Gate of Heavenly Peace and enter Chang'an Boulevard—reminders that the inspiration of the past continues to have meaning among the realities of the present, man-made or natural.

When my train, running ten hours late, brought me into Zhengzhou around midnight, all I wanted was sleep—maybe until the next afternoon and the next train. But my local guide made an irresistible suggestion: "In the morning, wouldn't you like to see the Yellow River?"

West of Zhengzhou is the "Great Bend" where the Huang He (Yellow River) shifts out of a southerly course and veers eastward. On the morning of Children's Day (June 1), truckloads of youngsters clogged the road to a riverside park. There, in the shimmering sunlight, we could hardly see the northern bank. Children shed their shoes and waded into the shallows. One or two "naughty little boys" (my guide speaking) shed *everything* and bellyflopped in the cool sandy ooze. The river looked benign; much too shallow for shipping, it moved imperceptibly, listless in the hot sun.

Like other mighty river systems of China, it can be capricious, threatening, devastating. Problems of controlling and conserving water have baffled engineers and defied solution for centuries. Rainfall, although abundant in China, is highly seasonal, 80 percent of it falling in summer.

Then, dry riverbeds overflow with surging floodwaters, mortally dangerous but much too precious to lose. The overpowering need to fend off
floodwaters, to supply irrigation works, and to provide transportation
long ago placed water conservancy at the heart of China's public works
projects and gave hydraulic engineers great influence.

Ancient mythology says that Yu the Great, son of Gun the First Engineer, was first to conquer the floods. His authority passed to successive
generations of human specialists. By the seventh century A.D. the imperial
Directorate of Hydraulic Control had a Sub-directorate of Fords, Ferries,
and Bridges. High prestige surrounded its Comptrollers of River and
Dike Works, who outranked its Officials in Charge of Sluice Gates.

Dedicated engineers and battalions of laborers frequently met their
match in the Yellow River. Rising in Tibet, it gathers loess in its easily
eroded middle course and reaches the eastern plain gorged with silt—as
much as 60 percent of its volume—that gives it the look and consistency of
oatmeal. As the water churns across the plain in flood season it drops as
much as a billion tons of sediment, and as it raises its own bed, men raise
levees ever higher beside it. Frequently it has broken free and inundated
the countryside for hundreds of miles, and it has even carved a new path
to the sea, destroying anything in its way. The Huang He has thus violent-
ly rearranged China's northeastern shoreline at least three times.

During centuries of attempts to tame the Yellow River, laborers have
dug canals to divert its waters. Sluice gates released the water at a gradual
rate, to enrich and not erode the fields. Still, the water had to flow rapidly
enough to scour the channel and keep it free of silt. The delicate problems of adjusting gradient occupied some of China's best minds for centuries, and inspired many learned tomes.

Put simply, one averts a flood by either of two ways: raise the dikes, or
lower the water. Contain natural forces; or adapt to their free play. Over
two millennia, arguments about these alternatives heated up to philo-
sophical debate of the highest order. The gods themselves championed
one cause or the other. Gun had been a dam builder (his efforts failed)
and Yu the Great had been a digger of channels (he succeeded).

During the third century B.C., Li Bing, administrator of a province
called Shu and a "deep channel" man, devised a system to regulate the
flow of the Min River—and, expanded, it serves the rich Sichuan basin today. Li directed his labor force in building an embankment that split the
river into inner and outer channels. The outer channel followed the original course to the sea. Li directed the inner channel onto the Chengdu
Plain—but only after cutting a passage through nearby Yulei Mountain.
The water thus diverted eastward was channeled through a system of
feeder canals, conduits, spillways, and lesser conduits to supply 2,000
square miles of farmland and serve five million people. Surplus water was

*FOLLOWING PAGES: Freight barges of cast concrete motor along a stretch of the
Grand Canal at Wuxi. Begun in the fifth century B.C., the waterway eventually
stretched more than 1,500 miles, linking five of China's major river systems and
providing transportation between the industrial north and the agricultural south.
Today it supplements the railroad network of the People's Republic of China.*

rerouted to the outer channel, and on downriver. Later it became the custom that in October, when the river was low, workmen made repairs. They put up a cofferdam of bamboo and mud, first in one branch of the canal, then in the other, and cleared the bed of silt and debris down to the level prescribed by Li and his son, who carried on his work after him.

So successful was the project that a grateful populace erected temples to Li Bing and his son and made regular sacrifices in their honor. Incense is burned before their statues even today.

Utterly different is the fame of the authors of the Grand Canal. First completed during the Sui Dynasty in the seventh century, the Grand Canal is China's only great north-south waterway. Originally it linked the southern port of Hangzhou with the capital at Luoyang, and much later with Beijing. Then, stretching more than a thousand miles, it connected five major river systems. It still ranks as one of the world's longest artificial waterways and as one of the great engineering feats of all time.

When I rode along the tree-lined Canal in Jiangsu Province, my escort, Li Jianping, regaled me with stories of the nefarious General Ma, credited in legend with supervising construction here. Ma is charged with extortion, avarice, all manner of corruption—even with ordering cooked infant served at lunch. Whatever the reality, that litany of evil deeds suggests the pain that has engraved itself on local memory.

By A.D. 589 the Sui Dynasty had reunited China after years of war. Much as the Qin Dynasty had utilized old walls, the Sui made use of transport canals to build a unified system between political centers in the north and the grain-producing south. By 605 a new link had been dug between the Yellow and the Huai Rivers. By 608 a new reach was ready to supply Chinese troops on the Korean border. By 610 the work was complete.

Building the Grand Canal confronted its engineers with novel and gargantuan problems. It was one of the first true summit canals—that is, it followed the contour of the landscape, literally making boats go uphill by means of an intricate system of sluice gates, ramped spillways, and locks. One 62-mile section alone needed 60 gates of varying design to cope with changes in elevation. And water was always in short supply in higher country. Feeder canals brought water from faraway rivers; great holding tanks stored it; gates fed it into the locks as needed.

I saw a new statue of Yu the Great presiding over the park by the Yellow River near Zhengzhou. In the south, in Shaoxing, his tomb attracts hordes of Chinese tourists. Near Mount Song in Henan, my guide had expounded at great length Yu's exploits as an engineer—including a tale of how, for one project, he had changed himself into a bear. Clearly the old sage is as well loved as ever. But my favorite comment on his role comes from the irreverent fourth-century philosopher Shen Zi, who observed

Masterwork of hydraulic engineering diverts waters of the Min River. Built in the third century B.C. and still in use, it divides the river with a man-made island. To the right, a canal called Neck of the Precious Bottle cuts through Yulei Mountain to irrigate more than 1,400 square miles today. The Dragon-Subduing Temple commemorates Li Bing, the official who began the project; a larger one above the bridge memorializes his son for finishing the work and thereby honoring his father.

that hydraulic engineers "did not learn their business from Yu the Great, they learned it from the waters."

With equal realism, Confucius is said to have scolded fellow countrymen whose houses or whose ancestral temples were overly ornate. The rafters of a proper ancestral shrine might be polished to dazzling luster, but if its builder were truly virtuous, the roof should be made of thatch. A competent ruler would no more encumber his kingdom with the cost of grandiose architecture than he would put a yoke on a warhorse.

Ideas of what was proper in public buildings had changed dramatically by early imperial times. After the third century B.C. great audience halls floated on lofty platforms, and palaces loomed stupendous. Grand buildings became emblems of greatness. Their very gates could be structures of note. Lesser buildings—local shrines, noble residences, rural villas, even privies—imitated greater. Paintings and ceramic models suggest their quality. But because timber was the primary building material and because wood is subject to decay, insect pests, fire, and the ravages of war, few examples of truly ancient Chinese timber-framed construction have survived.

"If I want to see some of the best examples of ancient timber architecture, where should I go?" "Wutai Shan!" came the answer, without the slightest hesitation. I was talking with Professor Chen Congzhou, professor of architecture at Tongji University in Shanghai. Among the sacred peaks of Wutai, he assured me, I would find the oldest timber structures yet identified. Moreover, I would see splendid work from later periods.

Steam from the kitchen rises with incense and morning prayer among the temples of Wutai Shan. Gongs and drums announce the first service of the day for assembled monks, nuns, and the Buddhist faithful who flock to the place from as far away as Tibet, India, and Japan. This

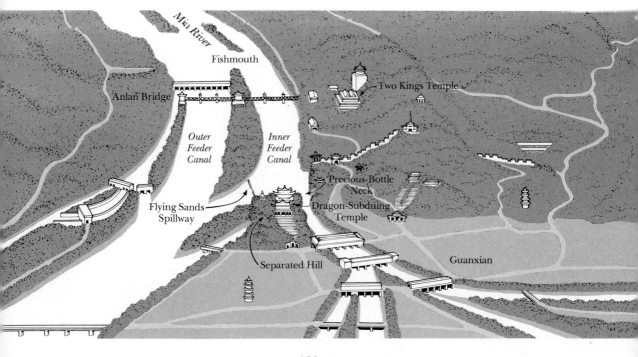

remote, chilly basin high in Shanxi Province has been a place of pilgrimage for more than a thousand years.

On the first morning of my visit, the singsong drone of voices chanting in the Great Buddha Hall was suddenly drowned in a brilliant cacophony of firecrackers, shouts, and the roughhouse jigs of young construction workers in the courtyard performing a "ceremony" of their own. With great good humor they were invoking whatever gods might be gracious enough to bring them luck as they broke ground for a new garden.

The temples share the forbidding hillsides with small farming villages. The religious communities, known as "yellow" temples (Tibetan) and "gray" (Chinese), do without such amenities as plumbing or heat, and seem to thrive on a hard way of life. The mountains look barren; their steep slopes seem to yield little but stone. I found it hard to imagine what feats of devotion brought building materials to this spot a thousand years ago. Nevertheless, this forbidding place presents the perfect somber setting for brilliant gems of the builder's art.

When you look at a traditional Chinese hall or temple, even (or especially) from a distance, certain characteristics impress the eye. These buildings are low, as though embracing the land out of which they seem to grow spontaneously. The most striking feature is almost always the roof. Glistening with layers of glazed ceramic tile, it is massive, and usually has overhanging eaves distinguished by a graceful upward sweep.

That distinctive arc comes from the intricate fit of the rafters. Western roofs usually owe their shape to straight timbers sloping from ridge to eave. Traditional Chinese builders, however, employed rows of short rafters that met end to end at a slight angle, thus making the roof somewhat concave. At each end-to-end joint, the rafters rest on purlins (supports running the length of the building). The purlins, in turn, are held up by columns set on a stone base. The concave surface holds its tiles securely, rendering the surface watertight, and the sweep of the eave conducts rainwater away from the foundations beneath. The "curve" we see, therefore, is an optical illusion produced by a series of neatly made angles.

A roof thus constructed is immensely heavy, with members extending well beyond their supporting columns. Ancient methods of coping with such weight have produced one of the most distinctive of all Chinese architectural forms, and one of the most ingenious. The Chinese devised a system of brackets and levers that they call *dou gong* (literally, blocks and arms). Western builders crown a column with a weight-bearing capital; instead, the Chinese set a block on the column. Each block holds a set of upward-curving arms. These arms, in turn, hold smaller blocks, each of which bears another set of arms with an even longer reach.

In addition to this balancing act of blocks and arms, a third element was often introduced, an angled, lever-like beam called an *ang*. The ang balances on a purlin like a seesaw on its fulcrum. As the ang receives weight

Guanyin, goddess of mercy revered by Chinese Buddhists, raises a hand in benediction at the Dule monastery in Jixian, near Beijing. Ten small heads on her crown signify her nature: all-knowing, therefore compassionate. The clay statue, brilliant in polychrome, stands 52 feet tall—largest image of its kind in China.

from the top, its lower end (its "beak," the Chinese say) rises to support the overhanging eaves.

On Wutai Shan one marvel competes with another in art and splendor, but for me, the place that most compels the imagination is the Nan Chan Si (Southern Meditation Temple), not on the peak but in the foothills. Nan Chan is simple, almost drab compared with the peacock display of its neighbors farther up the mountain. It is also older than they, built in 782 and considered the oldest timber-frame hall surviving in all of China. It is small—not important enough, perhaps, to warrant destruction during the purge of the 840s. (In those years the reigning emperor destroyed the power of the Buddhist establishment, and most of its temples with it.)

Nan Chan Si rests on a terrace overlooking neat squares of farmland in the valley. Small clutches of farmers gather in the garden for conversation. Simple of contour, the hall is spare in a way that Westerners associate with "things Japanese." The roof is dignified by a pair of spectacular ornaments; at opposite ends of the ridge, beak-shaped, they face each other like two hawks staring a rival down. The brackets are huge, each set about half the height of its supporting column. They are beautiful, and obviously functional; these blocks and arms make very clear what work each piece has to perform—indeed, has been performing for the last 1,200 years.

The interior, as in many one-story halls, has no ceiling to prevent full view of the elements that strengthen the roof of the sanctuary. Below, serene bodhisattvas float on lotus leaves while severe guardians, boldly modeled and painted, scowl at any who might be so irreverent as to do harm to the temple, to the solitary monk who lives here, or, I suspect, to the caretaker who smiles on guests and prunes the roses.

Like other major enterprises in China, building was subject to bureaucratic oversight. In A.D. 1103 the Song government published an elaborate codification of construction standards, bringing together all accepted practices. That document, the *Ying Cao Fa Shi*, described in detail the correct proportions for each element from basal platform to ridgepole. It established standards and grades for everything—even the parade of ceramic animals that was beginning to march along rooftops. It made possible a kingdom-wide system for modular construction, with standardized, prefabricated parts, easily utilized in proportions suitable for official, religious, or private structures.

Yet the Song code did not inhibit change or the play of imagination. Custom and architectural vocabulary permitted a blending of regional and cultural themes, nowhere more obvious than in the *ta*, or pagoda.

As tomb models and splendid murals show, the Chinese have been building towers since very ancient times—guardhouses and signal towers, it seems. With the introduction of Buddhism from "the West" (as the Chinese called India), powerful new ideas left their imprint on architectural forms. The evolution of the Chinese pagoda and its relationship to the Indian stupa are subjects for much academic debate. The fact remains, however, that pagodas stand today as testimony to a persuasive new religion and the effect of its iconography on a traditional Chinese form.

The timber pagoda of Yingxian, so splendid on the plains of Shanxi Province, so intriguing in miniature at Beijing, is the last remaining example of the pagoda constructed entirely of wood. It is octagonal (probably reflecting the eight-pointed compass of many Buddhist sects); its five stories, plus mezzanines and balconies, offered a grand opportunity for variations in bracket sets. It includes no fewer than 56 distinct combinations of dou, ang, and gong. In tribute to Indian forms, a wrought-iron *sha,* or finial, rests atop the pyramidal roof, bringing the overall height to an impressive 183 feet.

Once part of a considerable monastery, this pagoda enshrines noble and ancient statues on each uncluttered story. I especially admired the four Buddha figures, seated facing outward, calmly contemplating the surrounding plain. The great tower itself is the serene survivor of many earthquakes, its only evidence of strain a slight tilt to the northeast.

Early pagodas made of brick or stone might be short, squat, and square, or tall and bulbous; they might resemble a step pyramid or a goblet upside down. Whatever their form, they often *(Continued on page 192)*

Completed about A.D. 984, the Hall of Guanyin gives serenity today to a public park. Timber construction has proved its soundness in this famous shrine. The hall has withstood at least 28 major earthquakes, including the Tangshan disaster of 1976 and a quake in 1679 that leveled every other building in the district.

Cutaway views reveal techniques of ancient Chinese timber construction as prescribed for a Song Dynasty temple. Columns support the roof and the principal framing; walls—as in modern skyscrapers—carry little weight but their own.

Diagrams above contrast a western roof frame (top) with the Chinese type. In the West, braced rafters running from ridgepole to eaves distribute the weight to load-bearing walls. In China, sets of short rafters rest on round purlins, beams running the length of the building. Wooden brackets balance the load and transfer it to the columns. Built of terra-cotta tiles set in mortar over layers of planks resting on bamboo, the Chinese roof weighs much more than a western one. The builder puts that weight to good use with the diagonal beam called an ang, or beak (opposite, upper). The ang balances like a seesaw on a block centered within a set of brackets. As the roof weighs down one end of the beam, the other automatically rises to brace the heavy, overhanging eaves. These protect walls and foundations from damage by rainwater.

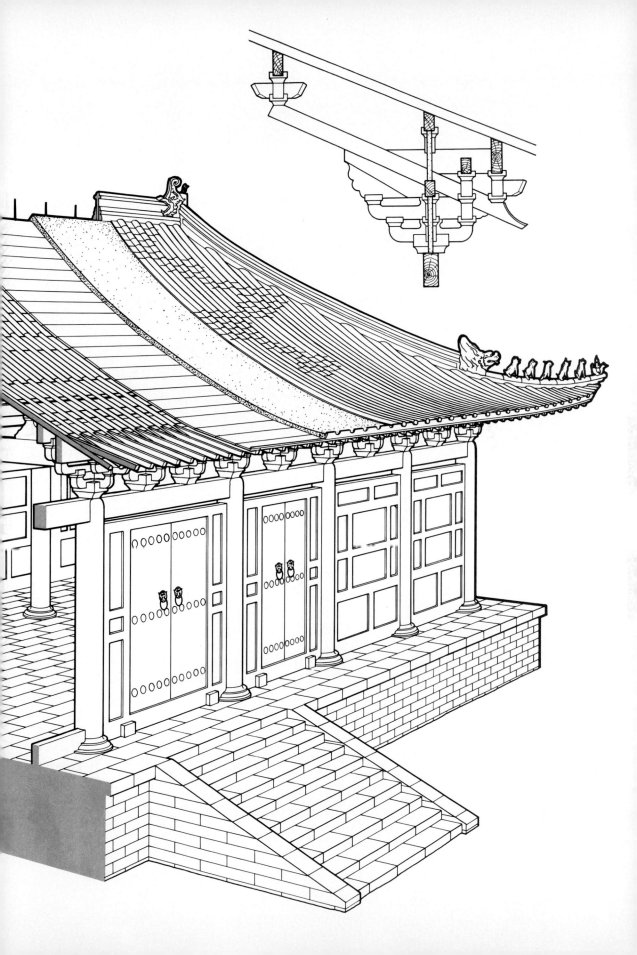

Layered tier upon tier to the sha, *or spire, one of the twin Kaiyuan temple pagodas (opposite) rises more than 158 feet at Quanzhou in southeastern China. Rectangular windows and arched doorways, alternating from story to story, admit light to interior stairs. Built in the mid-13th century, both pagodas mimic in stone the curved eaves and bracket-topped columns refined through centuries of earlier wooden buildings. At right, the nearly 1,000-year-old Yingxian Pagoda in the northern province of Shanxi— China's only surviving pagoda built entirely of wood—stands 183 feet high. It contains a veritable catalog of structural form; one architectural historian counted 56 variations in its brackets alone. Many scholars believe the earliest Chinese pagodas, usually simple, one-story square buildings, evolved from the dome-shaped stupas—tomb mounds—of India, where Buddhism began. As the religion spread, Chinese believers pressed their architectural heritage into the service of their beliefs, for watchtowers and signal towers had risen above city walls for centuries. The resulting multi-storied pagodas remain a familiar element of Chinese landscapes.*

did double duty in the service of local spirits. Cities competed to build the most imposing tower, or indulged in such whimsies as constructing pagodas in honor of venerable writing brushes.

Profound devotion inspired the famous Great Wild Goose Pagoda of Xi'an. It was the heroic monk Xuan Zang, sanctified pilgrim of the "Journey to the West," who consecrated the original tower in A.D. 652 and, it is said, wanted it to resemble square masonry towers he had seen in India. In a monastery associated with the tower, at the eastern terminus of the Great Silk Road, he translated the books he had brought back from his long journeys in search of the Truth.

Soon in need of repair, possibly damaged in a local war, his tower was rebuilt in 701. The replacement is severe in design, each of its seven stories rising cleanly, diminishing in size. Only careful inspection of the brick reveals the "shadow" of brackets etched into an otherwise pristine surface.

Such painstaking and skillful work touched the lives not only of the elite but also of the humblest. No better example could be cited than the legacy of China's bridge builders. The far southwest, deeply cut by gorges, preserves splendid examples of early cantilever and suspension bridges. The north and the northeast tended to favor the graceful arch. The southeast, blessed with innumerable watercourses and abundant granite, preferred stone-beam bridges, some of them on a mammoth scale.

Eager to see one of the most fabled stone bridges of Fujian, I wandered one sizzling noonday through the narrow lanes of the village of An Hai. Its pavements, houses, and tall, soldier-straight fences reverberated with the *thup thup thup* of hammer on stone. Everything here seems made of granite and the entire population seems to be working it—beautiful pale granite of such a sheen that high noon sears the eyes.

My driver led me to a small shrine where candles burned before ancestral images: the entrance to the An Ping Bridge, one of the oldest, longest, and best preserved. Constructed in the 12th century, it crosses 5,000 feet with 360 spans. Remote and quiet, closed to all but pedestrian traffic, it seemed little touched by time. We sat and watched people crossing: farmers with shoulder-poles, farm women with baskets of produce, curious children. The bridge looked downright delicate in contrast to one I had seen, with gaps of 70 feet spanned by slabs weighing 200 tons. Western books evaded the question of how such structures were erected, dismissing it as a mystery. I wondered if the Chinese thought so too.

Professor Chen Si Dong, of the Fujian Bureau of Antiquities, graciously agreed to answer my questions if he could. He turned out to be a fervent bridge buff, and gave me an impromptu seminar. Once the bridges in Fujian were made of wood, he explained, to post-and-lintel design. That pattern was repeated when builders, probably for lack of lumber, began to work in stone. The great slabs were cut and mortised together. No mortar was needed for stability. Shuttle-shaped piers were designed to offer as little resistance as possible to the currents. The ponderous beams rested on them, end to end and three abreast.

"But how," I asked, "could a hundred-ton slab be moved?"

"Ice tides," replied Dr. Chen, with rising enthusiasm. "These bridges were built only on tidal estuaries, subject to especially high tides. And there were only two times a year when the great stones could be set into place: the autumnal equinox, when the waters are naturally at their

highest, and at the 'ice tide.' That's the spring flood, after the snow and ice in the mountains have melted. At those two times, on rafts made of junks lashed together, the great slabs were floated out to the piers and slid into place." (In later centuries, if a bridge needed repair, men built new piers to shorten the span and substituted lighter stones.)

In the north, the graceful arch of the stone bridge represents a different tradition; and for many observers it epitomizes the very best work of the ancient Chinese builders. It reveals elegant solutions to subtle engineering problems—often anticipating the West by centuries.

Western engineers usually braced the apex of a round arch with a keystone and wedge-shaped stones called voussoirs. The Chinese lined the arch with thin, curving stone slabs, fitted together without mortar. Load from the abutments and approach ramps tended to deform the arch; the designers countered this pressure with vertical masonry walls, built into the abutments on either side of the stream. These hidden "shearwalls" protected the arch from shearing stress and serious distortion.

As effective and as beautiful as the half-circle arch might be, it limited the width of a span, so that only narrow vessels could pass under it. It also meant a steeply arched roadway, tiring for man and beast. Chinese engineers were first to solve the problems of flattening out the arch, widening the span and lowering the roadway. The lower the rise in relation to the width of the span, the greater the strain on the crown of the arch. Many engineers have attempted such a span, only to see it collapse from the strain at the center. But since A.D. 610 the single-span, segmented-arch bridge at Zhaoxian has stood secure, the oldest example of China's success —and, for 14 centuries, by virtue of its beauty, an attraction for people who have traveled from distant provinces to admire it.

For China's builders, no task seemed so daunting that they could not take its measure. Yu the Great tamed the waters, and mere men emulated his feats. But mortals aspiring to imitate the gods paid a great price. However glorious the monument, popular memory whispers the secrets of its cost. In Suzhou, city of pagodas and gardens, dark stone slabs under Tiger Hill still cry out on rainy midnights, voicing the anguish of martyred workmen buried beneath. High above the Great Wall at Shanhaiguan, the widowed Meng Jian Nu still vainly searches the horizon.

In spite of the pain of their making, the works themselves still stand, justification for the pride they inspire, worthy monuments to the hands and the minds that toiled to give them shape. For all great works—whether of engineering, architecture, or of art—represent not only sacrifice but also determination, patience, and the creative genius that respects its own powers as well as those beyond itself. They inspire respect for the best, and awareness of the worst, of the civilization that produced them.

FOLLOWING PAGES: Models of contemplation during ten centuries of human turmoil, earthquake and flood, four images of the Buddha survey the windy, arid countryside of Shanxi Province from the third story of the Yingxian Pagoda. Footworn floors attest to the countless pilgrims who have sought inspiration there; the building's very existence pays enduring tribute to the technical skill and artistic insight of its builders, and the generations who preceded them.

Born in Minneapolis, WILLIAM ALBERT ALLARD graduated from the University of Minnesota. He is a member of Magnum, the international photographers' cooperative, and a contract photographer for the Society. Since 1964 he has had 16 articles published in NATIONAL GEOGRAPHIC, plus assignments for a number of books. In 1983 his *Vanishing Breeds* won the annual "Wrangler" Award for the Outstanding Western Art Book—the first photography book to receive this honor.

In 27 years on the Society's staff, DEAN CONGER has had 26 articles in the GEOGRAPHIC, for which he is an assistant director of photography. His coverage of the U.S.S.R., for the Special Publication *Journey Across Russia,* won a World Understanding Award in 1978, and a citation from the Overseas Press Club. The National Press Photographers Association named him Newspaper Photographer of the Year in 1955, 1956, and 1959, Magazine Photographer of the Year in 1981. A native of Casper, he graduated from the University of Wyoming.

Hawaii-born free lance RICHARD A. COOKE III holds a B.A. in fine arts from UCLA and a graduate degree in architecture from the University of Oregon. He has had varied "outdoor" photographic assignments for the Society, including a chapter in *Canada's Wilderness Lands.* Coverage of architecture is becoming a new specialty; for recreation, he builds houses.

RON FISHER was born and grew up in Iowa—"where hardly any building," he says, "is more than 80 years old." He attended the University of Iowa, where he majored in creative writing, and has been a writer and editor for the Society since 1970. His most recent book is the large-format, award-winning *Our Threatened Inheritance: Natural Treasures of the United States.*

British by birth and allegiance, NORMAN HAMMOND received his B.A., M.A., and Ph.D. in archaeology and anthropology from Cambridge University. Since 1977 he has taught at Rutgers. He is archaeology correspondent of *The Times* and a frequent contributor to the professional literature. Research has taken him to Ecuador, Afghanistan, and China as well as Mesoamerica, where the Society has sponsored his work. His article on Cuello, "Unearthing the Oldest Known Maya," appeared in the GEOGRAPHIC in July 1982; this is his first contribution to Special Publications.

Free lance BLAINE HARRINGTON III, born in Kansas City, Kansas, grew up in Denver and graduated from the Brooks Institute of Photography at Santa Barbara. He now lives in Bethel, Connecticut, but specializes in location work in Europe. This is his first assignment for Special Publications.

Born in Allentown, Pa., ANN NOTTINGHAM KELSALL earned her B.A. there from Cedar Crest College. She holds a graduate degree in East Asian history from the University of Maryland at College Park, where she has taught Chinese history and culture; she has also studied in Shanghai. At the Society she was a contributor to Asia sections of the cultural atlas, *Peoples and Places of the Past;* since 1984 she has been an area specialist on the staff of NATIONAL GEOGRAPHIC TRAVELER.

A native of Philadelphia, STEVE McCURRY majored in arts and architecture at Penn State. In eight years as a free lance, he has concentrated on travel and on war coverage. In 1980 he won the Overseas Press Club's Robert Capa Gold Medal for his work in Afghanistan; in 1985 he was the National Press Photographers Association's Magazine Photographer of the Year. This is his first assignment for Special Publications.

Free-lance writer, translator, and editor JOYCE STEWART, born in Utah, has studied at Scripps College, the University of California at Berkeley, and the University of Utah. She also attended the Université de Genève in Switzerland. She spent six years in Africa. Her assignments for the Society include a recent article on Rajasthan in TRAVELER. At present she is living in India, based in Calcutta.

GENE S. STUART received her B.A. from the University of South Carolina, her native state, with graduate study in archaeology and art history at the University of Georgia. Mesoamerican archaeology has figured in her life since 1958, and in her career at the Society—notably in her Special Publication *The Mighty Aztecs.* She has reported on topics as varied as the Ice Age art of Europe (in *Mysteries of the Ancient World*) and life in Samoa, Tonga, and Fiji today (in *Blue Horizons*).

Bold in design, sound in construction, the Colosseum still reminds the world of the greatness of Rome. Its site once held an artificial lake, a private luxury for Nero; shrewdly, the Emperor Vespasian devoted the site to public entertainment and had this huge structure built for games and spectacle. Its ancient name, the Flavian Amphitheater, recalls the dynasty of the donor and his sons, who succeeded him and who completed the work.

ACKNOWLEDGMENTS

The Special Publications Division acknowledges with pleasure the invaluable cooperation of many officials and agencies in nations that now act as guardians for great monuments of antiquity. The Division is equally grateful to the individuals and organizations named, portrayed, or quoted in this volume, and to those cited here, for their generous assistance during the preparation of this book: Richard Blanton, Richard L. Burger, Chen Xiuzheng, Cheng Te-k'un, Michael Coe, John Dore, Edward Dwyer, Susan Evans, Kent Flannery, Maguire Gibson, Cecconi Idolo, René Millon, Michael E. Moseley, Gregory L. Possehl, Jeremy A. Sabloff, Ken W. Scott, Su Wancheng, Gus Van Beek, Joseph Cho Wang, Wang Yingmin, S. Jeffrey K. Wilkerson, Yu Weiqing; Arnold Prima of Mariani & Associates, Inc.; China International Travel Service; the University of Pennsylvania, Tikal Project.

Library of Congress CIP Data

Builders of the ancient world.

Bibliography: p.
Includes index.

1. Engineering—History.   2. Architecture, Ancient.   I. National
Geographic Society (U.S.).   Special Publications Division.

| TA16.B85 | 1986 | 624'.09 | 86-5278 |

ISBN 0-87044-585-5 (regular edition)
ISBN 0-87044-590-1 (library edition)

INDEX

Boldface indicates illustrations;
italic refers to picture captions.

ADDITIONAL READING

The reader may consult the *National Geographic Index* for related articles. *Peoples and Places of the Past,* the Society's cultural atlas, is highly pertinent, as are the following: *Lost Empires, Living Tribes; Mysteries of the Ancient World;* George E. Stuart and Gene S. Stuart, *The Mysterious Maya;* Gene S. Stuart, *The Mighty Aztecs;* Loren McIntyre, *The Incredible Incas;* Bryan M. Fagan, *The Adventure of Archaeology.*

Other noteworthy titles follow:
Christopher Chippindale, *Stonehenge Complete;* I.E.S. Edwards, *The Pyramids of Egypt;* Peter Garlake, *Great Zimbabwe;* Jon L. Gibson, *Poverty Point;* Henry Hodges, *Technology in the Ancient World;* Kathleen M. Kenyon, *Digging Up Jericho;* Seton Lloyd, *The Archaeology of Mesopotamia;* Alfred Lucas, *Ancient Egyptian Materials and Industries;* Sylvia Pankhurst, *Ethiopia, A Cultural History;* Gregory L. Possehl, *Ancient Cities of the Indus;* Colin Renfrew, *British Prehistory;* John Ruffle, *The Egyptians,* R. R. Sellman, *Prehistoric Britain;* Sir Mortimer Wheeler, *Still Digging.*
J. J. Coulton, *Ancient Greek Architects at Work;* William L. MacDonald, *The Architecture of the Roman Empire;* John B. Ward-Perkins, *Roman Architecture* and *Roman Imperial Architecture;* K. D. White, *Greek and Roman Technology.*
Richard E. W. Adams, *Prehistoric Mesoamerica;* Norman Hammond, *Ancient Maya Civilization;* Doris Heyden and Paul Gendrop, *Precolumbian Architecture of Mesoamerica;* Mary Ellen Miller, *The Art of Mesoamerica;* John Lloyd Stevens, *Incidents of Travel in Central America, Chiapas and Yucatan.*
Graziano Gasparini and Luise Margolies, *Inca Architecture;* John Hemming and Edward Ranney, *Monuments of the Incas;* Michael E. Moseley and Kent C. Day, eds., *Chan Chan;* Henri Stierling, *Art of the Incas.*
A. L. Basham, *The Wonder That Was India;* Susan L. Huntington with John C. Huntington, *The Art of Ancient India: Buddhist, Hindu, Jain;* George Michell, *The Hindu Temple;* Andreas Volwahsen, *Living Architecture: Indian.*
Ancient Chinese Architecture, [Chinese Academy of Architecture]; C. Blunden and M. Elvin, *Cultural Atlas of China;* Kwang-Chih Chang, *Early Chinese Civilization;* Jacques Gernet, *Daily Life in China On the Eve of the Mongol Invasion 1250-1276;* James Kelly, ed., *The Grand Canal of China;* Liang Ssu-ch'eng, *A Pictorial History of Chinese Architecture;* Luo Ziwen et al., *The Great Wall;* Henri Masparo, *China in Antiquity;* Joseph Needham, *Science and Civilization in China,* vol. 1 and vol. 4 pt. 3; William Willetts, *Foundations of Chinese Art.*

Composition for *Builders of the Ancient World: Marvels of Engineering* by National Geographic's Photographic Services, Carl M. Shrader, Director, Lawrence F. Ludwig, Assistant Director. Printed and bound by Holladay-Tyler Printing Corp., Rockville, Md. Film preparation by Catherine Cooke Studio, Inc., New York, N.Y. Color separations by the Lanman Progressive Company, Washington, D.C.; Lincoln Graphics, Inc., Cherry Hill, N.J.; and NEC, Inc., Nashville, Tenn.